# Rome, Inc.

Beneath the surface of business affairs lies the drama of human affairs. In the Atlas Books–W. W. Norton Enterprise series, distinguished writers tell the stories of the dynamic innovators and the compelling ideas that create new institutions, new ways of doing business and creating wealth, even new societies. Intended for both business professionals and the general reader, these are books whose insights come from the realm of business but inform the world we live in today.

# Rome, Inc.

## The Rise and Fall of the First Multinational Corporation

## Stanley Bing

Atlas Books

W. W. Norton & Company
New York • London

For information about permission to reproduce selections from this book,
write to Permissions, W. W. Norton & Company, Inc.,
500 Fifth Avenue, New York, NY 10110

Manufacturing by The Courier Companies, Inc.
Book design by Chris Welch
Production manager: Amanda Morrison

Library of Congress Cataloging-in-Publication Data

Bing, Stanley.
Rome, inc. : the rise and fall of the first multinational corporation /
Stanley Bing.—1st. ed.
p. cm.—(Enterprise)
"Atlas books."
ISBN-13: 978-0-393-06026-3 (hardcover)
ISBN-10: 0-393-06026-8 (hardcover)
1. Rome—History—Humor.   2. Corporate state—Rome—Humor.
3. Parables—Humor.  I. Title.  II. Series: Enterprise (New York, N.Y.)
DG211.B56 2006
937.002'07—dc22
2005036128

**ISBN 978-0-393-32945-2 pbk.**

Atlas Books, LLC, 10 E. 53rd Street, New York, N.Y. 10022

W. W. Norton & Company, Inc., 500 Fifth Avenue, New York, N.Y. 10110
www.wwnorton.com

W. W. Norton & Company Ltd., Castle House, 75/76 Wells Street, London
W1T 3QT

1 2 3 4 5 6 7 8 9 0

# Dedication

To the Etruscans, for having the good sense to submit to the inexorable power of a corporate culture more powerful than theirs, and the role they subsequently played in making the Rome that conquered them a whole lot more classy. If you've ever been on the wrong end of an acquisition, you know how hard that can be.

To Julius Caesar, for showing what happens when a senior officer grossly overestimates the affection in which he is held by his subordinates.

To Augustus, for demonstrating that power and wisdom need not be mutually exclusive. Too bad his wife was a serial murderer.

To Nero and Caligula, not for how weird they might have been, but for how much they are like Forbisher, McDougall, and Wiener, not to mention half the guys on the twenty-third floor.

To the Huns, Vandals, Visigoths, Ostrogoths, and assorted other Goths, for never doubting that they could beat an adversary who was smarter, richer, and better organized. Theirs is the genius of entrepreneurs everywhere. More power to them!

To the glorious Italy of today, which would not have been possible had Rome not fallen.

And to Rome, for all that grandeur, sure, but also for blowing itself up, as we all do if we stay in the game long enough.

# Contents

The following are special instances of Caligula's innate brutality. When cattle to feed the wild beasts he provided for a gladiatorial show were rather costly, he selected criminals to be devoured, and reviewing the line of prisoners without examining the charges, but merely taking his place in the middle of a colonnade, he bade them be led away "from baldhead to baldhead." A man who had made a vow to fight in the arena if the emperor recovered, he compelled to keep his word, watched him as he fought sword in hand, and would not let him go until he was victorious, and then only after many entreaties. Another who had offered his life for the same reason, but delayed to kill himself, he turned over to his slaves, with orders to drive him through the streets decked with sacred boughs and fillets, calling for the fulfillment of his vow, and finally hurl him from the embankment. Many men of honorable rank were first disfigured with the marks of branding-irons and then condemned to the mines, to work at building roads, or to be thrown to the wild beasts; or else he shut them up in cages on all fours, like animals, or had them sawn asunder. Not all these punishments were for serious offences, but merely for criticizing one of his shows, or for never having sworn by his Genius. He forced parents to attend the executions of their sons, sending a litter for one man who pleaded ill health, and inviting another to dinner immediately after witnessing the death, and trying to rouse him to gaiety and jesting by a great show of affability. He had the manager of his gladiatorial shows and beast-baitings beaten with chains in his presence for several successive days, and would not kill him until he was disgusted at the stench of his putrefied brain. He burned a writer of Atellan farces alive in the middle of the arena of the amphitheatre, because of a humorous line of double meaning. When a Roman *eques* on being thrown to the wild beasts loudly protested his innocence, he took him out, cut off his tongue, and put him back again.

Suetonius
*The Twelve Caesars*


Among other things, Kozlowski allegedly spent $1 million in Tyco money on a birthday bash for his second wife, Karen Mayo, that featured an ice sculpture of Michelangelo's *David*—which sprayed vodka from its penis.

*New York Daily News*
September 12, 2002

# Preface
# Think Global, Kill Local

The first great multinational corporation was Rome, and its rise and eventual fall hold many lessons for we who are its inheritors. In these pages, we will describe, and then draw lessons from, the first corporate organization in human history. Others may claim that title, but they would be wrong. Genghis Khan and the Mongol hordes rampaging throughout Asia, killing, maiming, squashing, crunching, gobbling up territory and mutton with equal brutality and gusto? That's not corporate behavior. The Mayans, tearing out the hearts of their virgins to feed them, still beating, to their rather intolerant god? That's a little closer to corporate behavior, but just building a bunch of stuff and sacrificing those who can't defend themselves isn't all there is to corporate life.

No, corporations begin in a good idea, build themselves by providing products and services to those who need them, expand their areas of activity, evolving, creating more than they destroy, driven always by a central desire to do well and keep their executives happy. From the very beginning, Rome had one single, simple, great corporate idea—that anybody who was conquered by Rome, brought into the body of the business, was a Roman. Once you were acquired you were no longer Them. You were Us. Rome sold citizenship to the world. And how good a product that was, when much of the world lived in mud and died trying to grab a fish by hand out of a rocky stream.

To be a Roman! Particularly for middle managers in the musty little operations that eventually came under its control, that was seductive indeed, an internal marketing concept that did a lot to almost immediately alienate vice presidents of the Frank or Visigoth organization from their senior officers. What would you rather be? A director of strategic planning for Rome or a vassal of some guy with fur up his nose?

That was a rhetorical question. It is always better for middle management to be a small, delectable part of a snazzy multinational, rather than a big fat slug in a pile of pig slop. First of all, there's a lot more travel, the perks are better, you get to take an occasional bath in opulent surroundings and even, if you're lucky, meet the Caesar. In short, corporate life, no matter how tough it is, has its rewards, especially if death is the only alternative to membership. Just ask anybody who's tried to make it in the advertising business in the last ten years. If you're not one of the Romans, you're likely to be one skinny Hun.

# Rome, Inc.

# 1

# In Which Two Brothers Form the Beginnings of a Pretty Fair Mom-and-Pop Enterprise

All corporations begin in myth. Even small ones grow stories about their misty progenitors. Uncle Morty, who began his life without two nickels to rub together and now look! An entire chain of convenience stores running down the eastern coastline from Providence to Trenton! Ray Kroc, with a couple of bucks and a little burger stand in medieval California, slicing onions and flipping patties and thereby somehow creating the behemoth that would one day be able to boast on every one of its thousands of pit stops that billions and billions, and one day trillions, had been served. The young Bill Gates and Nolan Bushnell in a funky suburban garage more suited for the production of bad rock and roll than high technology, picking at their geeky acne and dreaming up the personal computer. Bill Paley, bored out of his skull in his dad's cigar business, deciding that the new medium of radio might be a decent way of moving product, and then asking himself why he shouldn't own the pipeline through which that product moved, and then wondering

what would happen if you linked those stations together to create a . . . what would you call it? A network?

These stories kick-start the internal engine of enterprise and
commerce, and move organizations to a unifying concept of
themselves, a sense of their own inevitability and import, which
at the very least gives them the ability to recruit employees who
will work for them for less money.

Rome's establishing saga begins with a few raggedy-ass shepherds living on a hill in the middle of nowhere, since everywhere
back then was the middle of nowhere. This small gaggle tended
their flocks and fought back the packs of wolves that roamed the
wild countryside.

Into this hostile environment came the original pop of the
future mom-and-pop corporation that would become Rome. His
name was Aeneas, and he was relocating from Troy after the
famously unfriendly takeover described in Homer. His son
founded a little roadside stand called Alba Longa, which grew big
enough to rate a struggle for control between a good king and a
bad king, who were brothers.

At any rate, the bad king got into power in Alba Longa, as they
quite often do in organizations large and small even today, and
the bad CEO was so dangerous to his brother that the brother
feared for his life and made himself kind of scarce, going on
innumerable road trips and important business elsewhere and
making himself otherwise difficult to fire.

The bad chief executive of Alba Longa was so darn bad that
he forced the daughter of the good king to become a vestal virgin. Vestals were important religious figures, but the one key

demand for continued employment was that they refrain from all sexual intercourse for the term of their lives. This probably worked as well for them as it seems to do for other celibate corporate cultures.

This vestal virgin, the daughter of the good executive, was, of course, exemplary, until she had either the good or bad fortune to attract the interest of Mars, god of war. Roman gods were lusty creatures, and as such were somewhat more likable than many others. And of course this wasn't the first time an awesome officer from headquarters popped into some local burg and left a weeping member of the support staff in a profoundly altered condition. Having taken a fancy to the vestal, the god wasted no time and, according to Tacitus, took her in her sleep. And so a pair of twins was born, with a virgin for their mom and a god for their dad, and their names were Romulus and Remus.

The vestal virgin—now a former vestal virgin, I guess—was the proud mother of the future proprietors of the new concern. Their presence, however, was not appreciated by the existing very bad CEO, who, when informed of their existence, threw their mother and themselves into the Tiber River, which was extremely cold and inhospitable, even to vestal virgins and offspring of divine entities.

Miraculously, she survived when her beauty was noted by the river god, who made an honest woman of her by marrying her, while her twins were heaved up on a riverbank where, the wolf population being what it was, a mother wolf was on hand to suckle the babies, who thrived and survived long enough to be adopted by the bad king's shepherd, who raised them to become exactly what the king had feared—his immediate doom and the next generation of senior management around there.

Thus they grew to manhood, these handsome, good, and gifted youths, going to school at Gabii and disporting themselves around the Alba court, where they were known as the sons of the shepherd, or possibly the swineherd, depending on who you believe, and getting on the nerves of the bad king's servants, but never drawing the attention of the king himself.

One day, there was some scuffle pertaining to the stealing of swine, or some other capital offense in those days, and Remus got together a bunch of youths to handle the situation. This gaggle was misinterpreted by the local authorities as a band of hourly employees intent upon the destruction of the CEO. Remus was hauled before the top guy, who immediately didn't know what to do with him.

Realizing there was something special about the young man, who was singularly beautiful, the bad chief executive, practicing what was even then the ancient art of delegation, referred the matter to his subordinates, who were at a loss as well. In the meantime, grandpa good guy, the once and future chairman, at that point a semiretired Jobs in the wilderness, popped up to exhort Romulus to go to the aid of his brother, which Romulus did, and before you know it Remus was free and the bad guy was dead and Alba Longa was once again in the hands of its rightful executive, their grandfather. And so was the first corporate shuffle complete.

Please note that in this story the paranoia of the evil executive is well founded. Paranoia almost always is, particularly in corporate cultures where the only severance offered to senior officers is their bodies from their heads.

Having been informed of their birthright, attended to business, and hoisted their grandfather back into his throne, Romulus and Remus went out on their own and moved down the road apiece, for two reasons. First, matters were settled in their hometown, and the only way they could rule in that place was to kill their own grandfather. This having been considered and rejected, the brothers had another problem—the enormous gaggle of soldiers, slaves, women, children, soothsayers, swineherds, and assorted riffraff who had glommed onto them during the recent corporate wars, all of whom were relatively footloose and ready for Freddy. What was to be done with this great resource which, if left unutilized, could quickly turn into a dangerous liability? The people of Alba Longa certainly wanted no part of this crew, particularly when the men began seizing local women for a wide range of purposes, even though, as Plutarch notes, "they certainly paid unusual respect and honor to those whom they thus forcibly seized."

It was now, in the very earliest days of the corporation, that its founders implemented a policy that was central in the growth and success of the enterprise. They opened their doors to any fugitive, traveling soldier, debtor, mendicant, or rootless castoff in the region, making available a temple for their sanctuary, protecting all and rejecting none, delivering not the slave to his owner nor the murderer into the hands of the police. And to each of these they offered a precious prize: citizenship in the new entity, or, in business terms, staff jobs for even the lowliest per diem employee or consultant. It is on such foundations that true loyalty is based.

This policy of offering citizenship to the conquered and the willing recruit alike ultimately made each acquisition accomplished by the corporation somewhat welcome to a significant number of the acquired, including, quite often, the senior management of the smaller, weaker, less well-dressed target corporation.

Before long, more than one thousand houses had popped up like overnight mushrooms on the Palatine Hill, and the brothers got to building their central location in earnest, in order to maintain this workforce and keep it cohesive.

This requirement for a central corporate office was recognized by the brothers R, as it has been by founders since then, and rendered the new company far greater cohesion and power, in the end, than the former great corporate entity in those parts, which had offices in Athens, Sparta, and other locations and, in the end, didn't know which way it was going, having gotten mired in the arts, philosophy, and the maintaining of the way things used to be.

Before long, there was a debate about where to begin the walls. The brothers began to annoy each other immediately. This may seem an excessive reaction to what should be the happy problems that attend expansion, growth, and mutual success. On the contrary. Then as now, fights about the size, shape, and configuration of office space have led to many a bloody duel.

So Romulus wanted to build headquarters in one place and Remus said the other. And Romulus wanted to do it this particular way, and Remus, of course, wanted to do it another.

Exasperated, Romulus figures, Hey, I'm just gonna move forward on this thing, if I have another meeting with Remus about it I'm going to friggin' kill him, even if he is my brother.

Romulus gets going on the project, getting to work right away on the first thing any good establishment requires: security, which in this case meant walls. The work begins. Excitement is high. My, thinks Romulus to himself, it's good to work alone! What a relief not to be constantly hounded by that obnoxious, opinionated, contrarian brother of mine! Romulus both revels and broods on this development, and the more he thinks about it, the angrier he gets. Here he is sharing his power and his name with this other guy, all he does is sit around shooting holes in all his ideas. And does he have any of his own? Not at all.

His city, Rome, will be great, the greatest city in the history of the world. It will have a vision, a destiny. It won't be some dump like the place his wacky brother would cook up. What would he call his copycat city, anyway? Reme?

The stories differ about what happened that fateful day Romulus lost his temper and divested the corporation of his brother. Some believe that Remus ragged on the size of the city's new walls, saying they were too low and, in some accounts, jumping over them derisively because they were so puny. Jokes about size and height never go over very big with highly competitive men. It is generally accepted that Remus jeered at his brother, who just couldn't take it anymore and knocked him upside his head. Perhaps he didn't mean to kill him. Let's decide to think so, even though such belief is belied by the rest of Roman history.

This was no violent aberration. In killing his brother so that constructive work could go on, Romulus was displaying all the elements of the true executive personality and establishing the corporate culture at the same time.

### The Executive Personality
- Intelligent, strategic, dynamic
- Many other wonderful characteristics, plus . . .
- Squirrelly with neurotic pride
- Prey to convulsive, uncontrollable anger
- Bad impulse control
- Ethical, but amoral
- Bold, decisive, creative
- Minimal sense of humor about himself

In that one swift act, Romulus became Rome. Just as Edison, Ford, and Jobs put an irrevocable brand on the corporations they founded, he established the way Rome lived then—from what people wore to when and what they ate, the times they went to sleep, how they spoke when proud or sad or angry, what they did on the road, all of it, Romulus set the tone for the thousand years that followed. He was decisive. He was extremely dangerous. He liked to build things, and to kill things, too. In his person, he balanced the twin forces of creation and destruction more than any other man of his time. Those are the qualities that made Rome work, along with a vicious appetite to do whatever was necessary to get the job done.

What they were selling now was the idea of Rome to the world. In the end of days, when that sense of mission was gone, it didn't matter how many troops you had, you were losers. Here, in the beginning, Romulus gave the company the one essential gift only a founder can provide: the concept of the corporation.

With that in their hearts and minds, they were already unstoppable.

# 2

# First Acquisitions and Other Rapes

So Romulus killed Remus and buried him on Mount Remonia, with the kind of fanfare corporations reserve for those they have truly screwed over, after which the eliminated are aggressively forgotten or minimized to the point of obscurity. He then sent for some local consultants to advise him on how to mount the kind of kickoff any great project deserves, a mix of hocus and pocus that, along with the actual activity of construction, builds the psychic along with the physical structure of the company.

First, the builders dug a huge round trench around what they estimated would be the common area where the greatest number of people would assemble. They then threw in the first fruits of the season, plus a bunch of other stuff deemed necessary for luck and success at that time.

The group then did a very important thing, brilliant, really, if you're considering the senior managers who came up with the symbol. It shows they were truly thinking long-term, reaching for the hearts and minds of every potential denizen of the new corporate center.

Every member of the building committee threw a clot of dirt into the trench, no ordinary soil at all, but a handful that came from each man's native land. Think of the moment. All these grizzled survivors, veterans of innumerable battles, seasoned campaigners all, far from home, silently tossing a piece of their deepest hearts into the organizational myth. Is it any wonder that this produced a corporation that lasted a thousand years?

They called the trench "Mundus," the center of the world, and they built out from it. I once attended a corporate retreat where the entire senior management of the company was forced to build sand castles in their bathing suits. It seemed stupid at the time, but when we were done you could feel the unity coursing through the group. (This was possibly also attributable to the amount of wine we were all passing around at the time.)

Keeping the emotional ball in the air, Romulus then fitted a bronze plowshare to his plow and, yoking together a bull and a cow, drove the plow around the magic circle that had been created. (The symbolism of the bull and cow is somewhat obscure.) During the plowing, Romulus gave instructions that all the earth that was kicked up should be turned inward toward the city, thus keeping the corporate vibes they were generating contained within its structure, without a drop being allowed to leak out. An exception to this sanctification effort was made for openings that would hold the gates of the new corporate center, since it was assumed that many unclean—that is, non-Roman—beings could be expected to pass through those portals.

Rome was thus begun, as all great enterprises since, with a lot of spiritual and religious hooey attached. God, who is presumably busy in many locations, takes the time to make the corporation—or the football team or rapper, for that matter—sacred, and the source of all good things afterward. When the Wizard of Menlo Park finally found the right filament to create the lightbulb, he didn't say, "Look what I've done." He said, "What hath God wrought." This excuses a lot of sins both past and future.

So here we have Romulus, unencumbered by his obnoxious and opinionated partner, his headquarters rising most satisfactorily, but surrounded somewhat uncomfortably by a large, underemployed (and to some extent unemployable) workforce of lusty lumpen proletariat who had nowhere to go but up in status and comfort. Something needed to be done, and quickly.

While he was building his city, Romulus made a bunch of very wise decisions that set out the corporate culture that was Rome for its entire meaningful life span. First, he required all males old enough to make any trouble to join the army. He then organized the army into legions of three thousand foot soldiers and three hundred horse, and gave them cool uniforms to wear so they felt good about themselves.

This militarization of the young left older men with nothing to do. So Romulus, proving once again that he was certainly no dummy, chose one hundred of the most eminent old troublemakers and gave them jobs as lifetime consultants to the new corporation.

He called them the fathers of their nation, patricians, and set them up with a really cool clubhouse to hold their meetings in, a place where they could talk to their hearts' content and do important things indeed—as long as those crucial activities posed no threat to the chairman. And so they became the Senate, which was such a good name that we use it still. (There are those who believe that the one hundred were called patricians, by the way, because they were the only guys around who actually knew who their fathers were.)

In this way Romulus created that corporate bond between the common people who labor for the nation-state and those who most directly benefit from their labor—the patrician class—and invented the myth, still quite active in all successful organizations, that management exists to protect its employees.

Love of the masses for their patricians is essential. But it is not enough. The Capitoline Hill, which was the most impressive of the promontories that were to make up the new city, was a fine base for the outlaws and fugitives who then were passing for city fathers. There was a fertile wilderness to tap for food and shelter. But food and shelter are not enough to hold a group of people together with the force necessary to create a corporation.

Several such needs reared high in importance to the newly empowered chairman. The first was already under way—the construction of a corporate center, one which he could pretty much design for himself now that his chucklehead brother was out of the way. His second and equally important objective was the peopling of this headquarters with individuals who were likely to stay put for a while, be loyal to the company within current standards on the subject, and not kill him if and when things got difficult, at least not right away. Essential in this regard was making Rome a place where the family unit could exist and thrive.

Most great corporations that intend to stick around for a while are very big on families. Have you ever wondered why? Why is it that even the most hard-hearted fire-breathing CEO sends letters to the homes of his employees now and then? Why do places that fire people at holiday time still have Christmas parties and summer picnics, and woe to the employee who skips one? Why does senior management at successful corporations make spouses dress up in silly black tie and gowns for evenings out on the town with "the team" that strain all human levels of tolerance for everybody involved?

It's simple. Once a worker's family sees itself as part of the effort, a different kind of bondage is established between wage slave and the executives who run his or her life.

There are corporations that break this mold entirely, of course. Microsoft, for instance, makes it virtually impossible for its soldiers to maintain a human lifestyle, thereby keeping its workforce young, exhausted, stoked on greed and ambition. This also makes it possible for the gigantic multinational to avoid pension costs that have brought down more traditional nation-states. At the same time, the lack of a family-friendly structure may also be one of the reasons why, in spite of all the efforts of its emperor to create a Roman hegemony over the known world, that company has yet to crush the barbarians in its path. I'm writing this on an Apple, for instance.

To create the family, even back in the dawn of history, you needed certain relatively simple things:

- Structures congenial to work, play, and social activity, with walls around them to keep out bad guys, just as contemporary office towers and residential buildings maintain security at their front gates to exclude mendicants, salespeople, and individuals who wish to leave menus for local Chinese restaurants, with varying degrees of success.

- Means of livelihood for men in need of money, so they do not have to rob and kill in order to sustain their work, play, and social activities. This involves a strategy of intense labor for the available workforce, which, in the case of all empires, means acquisition and conquest.

- Women. You really can't have a society without them. It is difficult, however, to attract women to a pile of mud in the middle of nowhere, particularly good-looking, cultivated women who live elsewhere in conditions that by any standard of the time had to be considered superior to what the new start-up was offering.

Thanks to his creation of the military and to an aggressive plan of construction that both built the city and employed the men, not dissimilar to the New Deal of the 1930s in Depression-plagued America, Romulus provided the first two things. But for the third, he would need to make a big fat acquisition that expanded the corporation's power base, revenue stream, and growth prospects in one decisive act.

This required more than just manpower. A culture dedicated to the pursuit of acquisitions must be aggressive, predatory, and convinced that its way of life is superior to the parties it envisions conquering. In the case of an entity like Rome, essentially an enclave of thugs, castoffs, and rejectees from more developed corporate entities, there was no reason to believe in such superiority or right to conquer. That didn't stop the new corporation from asserting that very right to rule over others more established and in some sense worthier than they, because Romulus and his executive team infused the male citizenry with the belief that their culture was destined to prevail.

In the case of the young enterprise, the local clergy was very helpful in providing a larger framework for current strategic thinking on war. Oracles were on hand to whip up the CEO with delusions of grandeur, informing Romulus that his city was destined by the Fates for tremendous success. With the gods on his side, the boss perfected his thinking and built his plan.

The answer the founder came up with was as brilliant as the conquest of Sears by Target, as bold as the takeover of Chrysler by Daimler, as risky as the plunder of Compaq by HP. It expanded the corporation's power base and solved the woman problem in one decisive act that created the potential for the male citizenry's permanent sexual, social, and domestic bliss and would keep them busy for the duration. In one act, Romulus introduced a full complement of desirable women to this smarmy male society and virtually ate an entire competitor.

He did so by merging the lust for acquisition with lust of a more primal nature and force, using an age-old tool wielded by those who wish to conquer more than the hearts and minds of their enemy. That tool is rape.

Up the road from the new and increasingly horny band of

Roman gypsies, tramps, and thieves lived a tribe called the Sabines, whom Romulus identified as the perfect target. Romulus let out that he had discovered a secret temple under the Circus Maximus, which was not a circus per se, with clowns and elephants, but a big circle where they had races and things. To celebrate this great news, he invited his friendly neighborhood Sabines to a massive spectacle, complete with fabulous sacrifices and public contests and sports and all kinds of entertainments. Things being what they were back then in the area of public diversions, this was a lot more interesting than watching goats mate and virgins dance around a maypole, and folks came from hither and yon to enjoy the spectacle being mounted by the new city, both to enjoy the show and to see the new corporate headquarters of Rome. Most visitors brought their families.

Romulus sat in the front row with the rest of his senior management, dressed in purple robes should anyone fail to understand who was the noise around there. The signal he had arranged was simple: when he rose and slung his robe over his shoulder, his men were to get to it. Romulus rose, and his men, armed and ready, their eyes glued on him for the sign, rose as one, drew their swords, fell on the Sabines, and grabbed their women, with a particular focus on the young, plump ones, if one is to believe Poussin.

For their part, the poor Sabines, who were unarmed, ran away to fight another day. Perhaps the best that can be said of the Romans is that they were not Mongols or AOL executives, but allowed the Sabines to survive once their immediate business objectives had been attained.

There are varying accounts of how many women were acquired in the move. One source says 30, another 527, and a third 683, all of whom were virgins but one, an unlucky married lady named Hersilia. And that, according to Romulus, was a mistake. They meant to take no man's wife, just women who would help build Rome and, in the end, force cooperation between the city and its neighbor.

The Sabines' hands were tied. Their daughters, presumably no longer virgins, were now controlled by Rome. So, swallowing their pride, Sabine senior management ventured to Rome for some diplomacy. They proposed a fair solution to the problem: Rome returns the women, a pact of benefit to Sabines and Romans alike would be forged.

Romulus said no thanks, he'd keep the women, but was not averse to a deal on the other points. There was lengthy discussion and Sabine consideration and even some attempts to take out Romulus by one of the opposing generals, who descended on Rome with no good intentions whatsoever. Romulus and his army met Acron and his army just outside corporate headquarters, at a suburban conference center. And Romulus had a suggestion. Hey, he said, why kill all these good men. I'll fight you, mano a mano, may the best man win and all that. And the other guy agreed. So Romulus called on the gods, as he liked to do, being a religious man and all, and smote the other upside his head, and then beat his army too in the subsequent engagement, and conquered his city, too, demolishing it, killing very few but leaving the homeless with but one place to go: Rome.

And so is a world-class corporation built.

True, the Sabines in their various cities continued to fight. And that's what Rome, with its growing resources and sense of destiny, wanted. The Sabine subsidiaries of Fidenae, Crustumerium, and Antemna joined against the corporate incursion into their culture, were defeated, gave up their property, and were transformed into Romans—reluctant Romans at first, and then proud citizens of the greatest entity in the known world, one that was clearly on the way up.

It turned out that when he wanted to be, Romulus wasn't a bad guy at all. The lands and property he seized from the Sabines were distributed to existing Roman citizens—giving the conquered something to aspire to—except the lands of those who had lost daughters in the unfriendly takeover. These families were permitted to keep their property.

Still, a fair cohort of enraged Sabines hung in there, got organized, and once again marched against Rome. The insurgency began well. Through the use of spies and misdirection, the Sabines fought their way to control of the Capitoline Hill. This quite understandably made Romulus angry, but there was very little he could do at that point except fume and prepare for the mother of all battles, which began almost immediately. First, the Sabines were decimated, but fought on. Then Romulus got a stone to the head and the Roman cause looked doubtful. Just as they were about to flee down the hill, Romulus woke up and, his arms raised to the sky, beseeched Jupiter not to let the home team down. This seemed to work and violence continued until both sides took a step back and prepared for what would come next, i.e., more killing, more bloodshed, more exhortations to gods who either were paying attention or not.

Then something interesting happened, something that is quite common in business situations but first manifested itself in this particular merger. The Sabine women, so forcibly and brutally acquired, found themselves caught between their fathers and brothers, angry Sabines all, and the men who had seized them by force and now were their husbands and the fathers of their children. They begged for the fighting to stop, with lamentations and weeping and, most certainly, the withdrawal of sexual favors for those who had come to enjoy them.

And so the war was ended. Romulus and the head of the Sabines, whose name was Titus, ruled the corporation together as co-chief executives until the latter was killed in battle under suspicious circumstances, as sometimes happens even among the best of friends.

This Rape of the Sabine Women shows all the characteristics of a contemporary unfriendly takeover—one that succeeds, unlike the vast majority, which collapse into continual warfare and chronic nonsynergistic dysfunction, as ITT decomposed after all the brilliant moves of CEO Harold Geneen succeeded in creating a Frankenstein of a company that lumbered off into ignominy. The good ones look different, and follow the Sabine model pretty closely.

Step One: Rape. The acquiring party moves to fill an obvious gap in its infrastructure by seizing another entity and carrying it off to its boudoir. In this way, HP took Compaq, which gave them the capability to make cute, entry-level mediocre computers. Without that, HP was stymied. With it, they could go on to build their stock price and make headlines in true Roman fashion. Of course, HP was a little less humane to the employees of Compaq than Rome was to the Sabines.

Step Two: Lots of fighting. At HP, there was internal screaming that nearly tore the entire company in two for a long time. My old company was acquired by an unfriendly mass of trolls in the early 1980s. We didn't like them and we didn't cooperate with all their McKinsey nonsense until it became quite apparent that those who didn't talk the talk were not going to get the opportunity to walk the walk.

Step Three: Intercourse. At that point, much like the Sabine women, we fell in love with our captors. We went to their retreats. We attended their goofy meetings about Excellence and pondered their org charts and pretty soon we weren't divided into Us and Them anymore, we were just all a big mass of people who were sick of the divide and ready to get with the program.

Step Four: Marriage. And then it came to pass that our leader, to whom we were loyal, was given a big fat title and a lot of power, much as Titus the Sabine found himself coruler of Rome, at least for a while. We were happy in the bosom of the new corporation. The old guys had our revenues and operations to play with. Of course, our little Sabine village was gone, but then in the end everything goes, doesn't it? Even Rome?

After the death of Titus, and for the rest of his term, Romulus served alone, until the day he reportedly disappeared in a storm

and was carried to heaven, where he became a god to be worshiped much as we today worship Thomas Watson, Sam Walton,
Walt Disney, or Ronald Reagan, leaders who, for better or worse,
left the permanent impression of their characters on the corporations they led to world domination.

# 3

# The Republic

## An Ode to the Well-Run Corporation

After Romulus came a whole bunch of other CEOs who did a fair job of pursuing the Great Man's agenda of expansion and cultural hegemony over the known world. There were good ones and bad ones, but none whose control over the enterprise built the office of the chairman itself to the point where it was not replaceable by a less personal concentration of power. Eventually, the executive center did not hold the corporation together as effectively as middle management could, and the Republic was born.

The guys that came after Romulus were like those who served under George Washington, or Steve Ross. They did great things, of course, but the high point of their lives had been serving under the big dog. A lot of their work was doing line extensions on the basic brand established by the Dude.

They were busy, don't get me wrong. Romans are always busy. They invented their religion, which made about as much sense as anybody else's, and borrowed, the way the Chinese do now, the content without obtaining licensing agreements from its authors, in this case the Greeks. They reinvested and built up some of their really cool institutions, like the college of vestals, featuring a large number of virgins, possibly the biggest in history before the foundation of Smith.

In subsequent years, the kings extended Rome's grasp to all of Latium and founded the ports that would open the corporation to global resources and conquest. The Etruscan leadership moved in shortly thereafter, and did a good job of things for a while. The Etruscans were very mysterious. Nobody knows a lot about them. While they ruled Rome we see a lot of kings named Tarquinius, a name that has now fallen into disuse but was then quite popular. The first, Tarquinius Priscus, made his mark by building the first significant temples and, more importantly, the first sewer system in history, the Cloaca Maxima. With the Circus Maximus already providing quality family fare to the multitudes, we see that the new corporation well understood two of the primary urges of all civilized beings, even in our own time— the desire for on-demand entertainment and a decent-smelling place to rest one's head at the end of a long day.

But oops. Just as the Etruscans were getting things rolling, here comes a bona fide Roman again, Servius Tullius. Can you imagine the high fives that went on among the Latin middle management when their guy got in there? Upon getting the corner office, this Tullius immediately built a great wall to keep the Etruscans out, just as the guys at CBS tried to thwart Ted Turner's incursions in the 1980s by surrounding themselves with Tisches. This apparently didn't work very well back then, either, because the next king, in about 534 B.C., was an Etruscan again—Tarquinius Superbus, another great builder, as you can tell by the fact that he named himself Superbus. I've known a lot of egomaniacs in my time, but none has had the temerity to brand himself with that kind of flair.

Superbus's great misfortune, and that of the Etruscan civilization itself, was the loutish Tarquinius Sextus, his son, whose lust resulted in a permanent regime change.

The story goes like this: One day the sons of the Etruscan king of Rome, the aforementioned Superbus, are hanging around at Ardea, a city the army is then besieging. Besieging being rather boring work, the young men find themselves at sixes and sevens, talking about things employees of the corporation have talked about since the first rock smote the first Paleolithic brainpan. And of course they are drinking.

Here they are, drunk and full of food, after a good supper at the house of a well-to-do friend of a friend, and they start talking about their wives, and each naturally extols his own in full and fulsome praise. Finally, their host, a fine young fellow named Conlatinus, who is not the son of the king, it should be noted, says, Hey, I'm sure your wives are virtuous and all that, but nobody beats my wife in that department, and if you doubt it why don't we just get up on our big old horses there and pay each of them a surprise visit and see what's what.

So the big old lusty Roman hotshots, the sons of the king and their working-class host, hit the road, three sheets to the wind, and pop in on their respective spouses.

It was getting dark in the Roman hills when the riders pulled up at each of their circular driveways. At the homes of the daughters-in-law of the king, they found each wife getting set for a night on the town, whatever that meant in those days, doing their hair, anointing, hanging with their nubile pals getting set for a feast, stuff like that.

The home of Conlatinus was different. Even though it was night by now, his virtuous wife, the matron Lucretia, sat spinning, which was probably the primary domestic duty of the Roman spouse in those days. As opposed to loitering about with a bunch of rich babes doing their nails and kibitzing, she was with her servants, working, in the middle of the atrium.

Needless to say, everybody was very impressed with Conlatinus's virtuous wife, and recognized him to be the winner of their little game. It was the duty of the winner to invite the king's sons in for further wassail. The excellent young wife did so, even though, one may imagine, she might have been a little perturbed at the prospect of entertaining her husband's drunken friends at that hour unannounced.

The young men spent a few hours at the house, drinking and playing cribbage, or quoits, or whatever it was drunken Roman besiegers did before the invention of video games, and then went back to the camp. While they were at their host's abode, though, the king's son, Tarquinius Sextus, took a shine to the wife of his friend, excited by both Lucretia's beauty and her goodness, and determined to come back later and do something to ruin it. The night of fun being ended, they went back to the camp and fell asleep in their own vomit, that then being the style, as it is today on many college campuses.

A few days later, the nasty prince went back to the home of Conlatinus with a sympathetic friend to watch his back, and was received politely by the worthy Lucretia, who, after explaining that her husband was away at the office, invited the king's son in for a bite to eat and a spot in the guest room.

In the middle of the night, when he was sure the house was asleep, the young noble unsheathed his sword, went into his hostess's chaste chamber, and placed the tip of his cold, hard weapon against her left breast.

A conversation ensued, back and forth, with entreaties and threats of death on one side and staunch, righteous resistance on the other, until the royal seed came up with an effective argument: If you do not submit, he said, I will kill you and lay you beside the dead body of a nude servant, so that everybody will think you died during an act of adultery. With this, presumably keeping in mind that her co-respondent would be the son of the king and difficult to gainsay, Lucretia gave in.

When the royal rapist had departed, Lucretia, understandably hysterical and upset, sent for both her father and her husband. They found her in her chamber, sobbing for her lost honor. When she saw them, she told them what had happened and who had returned the hospitality of their house with shame. "My body is soiled, although my heart is still pure, as my death will prove," she said, adding, "My sorrow will also be his if you are real men."

Her husband and father argued with her, saying that the soul was not sullied if the body was not a willing participant—a line of thought that has failed to assuage the pain of many a rape victim before or since.

"I will absolve myself of blame," Lucretia said, "but I will not free myself from punishment. No woman shall use Lucretia as her example in dishonor."

Then she did as many a Roman seemed to find it easy to do in those days, drawing a dagger from beneath her robe and slicing her heart in two, she died amid the lamentations and cries of the men who loved her.

I will interrupt our corporate history here for just one moment to wonder how it was so seemingly easy for members of this culture to plunge sharp objects into themselves, let alone total strangers. I don't know about you, but I get annoyed when I slice myself shaving, and somewhat alarmed at the sight of my own blood. Yet it is impossible to march forward through any segment of Roman history, no matter how slender, without finding one citizen or another plunging cold steel into his or her own rib cage, drawing daggers across their own throats, and so forth. Such capabilities must be acquired through specific teachings that are now lost in the mists of time. Now, I suppose, people drink themselves to death, or work themselves into an early grave, or even jump off an occasional office tower. But the willingness, nay, the propensity, of Romans to stab and hack themselves and others was an absolutely crucial factor in the success of the corporation.

At any rate, the rape and subsequent suicide of Lucretia became a symbol and driver of a wholesale restructuring of the state. For accompanying Conlatinus was his friend, Junius Lucius Brutus, who took the knife from Lucretia's breast and, holding it in the air, dripping with blood, made a little speech.

"By this blood, which was so pure before the crime of the prince, I swear before you, O gods, to chase the king, with his criminal wife and all their offspring, by fire, iron, and all the methods I have at my disposal, and never to tolerate kings in Rome evermore, whether of that family or any other."

Thus an unacceptable act led to wholesale reforms. One may hope the same for places like Tyco, the New York Stock Exchange, and even General Electric, where highly effective, charismatic leaders have been replaced by a bureaucracy that, while it is less interesting to future historians, may run the place with equal if not superior wisdom.

The fable and lesson of Lucretia meant as much to the Romans as the Boston Tea Party did to the young American bourgeoisie, offering a heartfelt cry for honor, justice, and process against the exercise of force by hereditary tyranny.

The past was full of bowing and scraping. Before them, or so they hoped, lay a future of laws, not men, of discourse, not blood. That destiny would be achieved through the establishment of a rational organization with a comprehensible reporting structure and clear guidelines and policies, goddammit.

Thus Rome became free of its kings and entered a five-hundred-year golden age of rational management that got a hell of a lot done.

The Senate, first established by Romulus, was the heart of the new corporate enterprise. The word *Senatus* comes from the Latin *senex*—"old dudes"—which makes the Senate, literally, a "council of old dudes," which is a pretty adequate description of my corporate board, and probably yours, too.

At first, as we know, it was made up of one hundred patricians, a brilliant way of co-opting the ruling class and making it a willing and domesticated part of the senior management of the company. Somewhat later, nonaristocrats were also drawn into the body, similar to the practice, these days, of drafting internal senior management to take part in board meetings, not simply helmet-haired gray-bearded elders. The lower house spoke for the unwashed employees, and at times was ruled by them, in the form of the famous and highly effective mob.

Most importantly, the Senate empowered the chief legal figures, their corporate consuls, to name a dictator in extraordinary circumstances, which most often involved the army in one way or another. This created a legal framework for dictatorship in times of strife, which turned out to be a pretty continuous state by the time the Republic had been around for a few hundred years.

Romans both rich and poor adored their Senate, and were willing to die to protect it. They knew that when the Senate fell, or was eroded, or crushed, the whole organization would be the worse for it, but most particularly the merchant class and other working affluent who didn't want to obey an intrusive, divinely enthroned monarch.

This is not to say that everybody simply lay down in front of the nearest guy in a pleated curtain. There were many who sought to contain the power of the fattest. The first challenge to Senate dominance came from within, as the various constituencies of management worked out how things would operate in the new, kingless pecking order.

The problem was the general economic situation. Things were

so bad that common people routinely ended up owing money to the rich. It was not the same as it is now, where the greatest punishment for debt might be repossession of your vehicle and a polite bankruptcy. In Rome, debtors were sold into slavery. There were few protections offered to those without connections and family pedigree, and a considerable amount of resulting nervousness among struggling employees of the company and its non-aristocratic middle management, which now found, in the absence of a strong central executive presence, that they needed protection from their new bosses, who were just as dangerous to them as the old one had been.

The word "plebeian" conjures up images of guys sitting around a scratched oaken table in the local tavern, eating a haunch of something and picking their teeth with a pitchfork. All that is truly conveyed by the name, however, is a group of people who were not born into families that made a difference in the social hierarchy. If you were not an aristocrat born with a silver chalice in your mouth, you were a plebe, and that was that. The amount of money you might have managed to assemble did not make a difference. If you're a citizen of Bombay at this time, a big bankroll cannot buy an upgrade in caste. The daughter of a wealthy rug merchant in Queens similarly can't purchase the right to be presented at the debutante ball. And a pile of gold in ancient Rome didn't mean a thing when it came to the acquisition of political power. So the plebes, many of them rich landowners, soldiers, merchants of consequence, people like you and me, looked at what kind of leverage they might have.

It was the leverage wielded by workers everywhere and at all

times—the simple weight of the labor that they do. These were
the soldiers, sailors, merchants, and artisans who made the life
of the enterprise possible. Bosses have a tough time figuring out
their mission when they have nobody to delegate to. Many of the
plebes actually had just as much money and means of using it as
your average senatorial executive; as in the American Revolution
several thousand years later, this was not an uprising of the
lumpen. This was the blunt assertion that the democracy of capital would to some extent find expression in the way the state was
run. They could also quit anytime they wanted to, and senior
management would have to deal with them as a serious force—
lest work on ongoing acquisitions, constructions, pillages, and
public projects grind to a halt. And then? No Rome, Inc., which
increasingly was built on the presumption of continual ferment
and growth.

Between about 500 B.C. and 300 B.C., the Republic suffered
five strikes of its middle-management cadre, a phenomenon
known as the Conflict of the Orders. In the first, the plebes simply pulled out of Rome altogether and lodged themselves on a
hill a few miles north of corporate headquarters. This left the
executive ranks with a serious problem. They could cling to the
status quo and suffer significant loss of revenue and decline in
the quality of aristocratic life, or they could deal with the striking workers in such a way as to bring them back to work without
seriously impinging on their own power too egregiously in future.

In other words, in addition to inventing the multinational corporation, Rome invented the strike as a means of forcing change
to that infrastructure.

The leaders of the plebeian union were tough, seasoned guys. For the most part they had a background in the military, as did most adult Roman males. They had experience in organizing campaigns. They had money to keep the strike going without suffering too much hurt. They were in some ways tougher than the guys who ran the corporation. They were formidable adversaries the ruling class of Rome had to do something about.

So the corporation instituted a bunch of reforms that gave the illusion of change without seriously threatening the primacy of their class.

- They recognized the right of the plebeians to hold meetings and elect leadership that would deal with the board of directors of the Senate and make middle management's needs and position on the issues known.
- They authorized the creation of a rational written document that expressed the bylaws of the corporation.
- The plebes were given the right to elect the chief executives of their lower body. These were the tribunes, and they evolved some meaningful powers over time as long as the threat of secession was made clear to the guys in the starched togas.
- The tribune of the plebes was also a kind of ombudsman to his class, with the responsibility to be of the people, to be in touch with those who had specific grievances, and to make those problems known to his betters.
- The tribune could also veto any corporate laws the senatorial board of directors wanted to implement; this provided a stopgap to executive abuse now virtually unknown in our day,

unless you ascribe the role of tribune to guys like Alan
Greenspan or Messrs. Sarbanes and Oxley.

Today, the moderating influence of the people is expressed not
within the body of the corporation itself, as it was in Rome, but
in the collective weight of shareholders and their sometimes
noisy representatives, who are only too happy to rise up and talk
to the *Wall Street Journal* or some humorless attorney general if
they feel the patricians on the board are getting out of line. This
is significantly less satisfying than chasing your elegant adversary
down the street with a truncheon, but almost as effective, particularly these days, when media profile is at such a premium.

The tribunes of the people also kept in close touch with the
class that was lower than they—the mob, making sure that the
underclass was placated when annoyed and aware that it, too,
had a means to address the power structure when need be.

Romans liked being managed by their aristocracy. They didn't
even try to gain entry to that elite club, at least for a long while.
They just wanted a piece of the management action, and that is
exactly what they received. Much less power than the bosses,
but enough to balance the social structure and allow all classes
within the city to get on with the business of Rome—facing the
rest of the world as a united entity at peace with itself, for the
most part, while content to be at war with everybody else.

To get the bylaws going, in 451 B.C. the Senate named ten
patricians to work out a simple code everybody could live with.
They came up with ten tables, Romans being very big on order
and things coming in groups of ten. Apparently, the aristocratic

source of these regulations was noted by one and all, and a further effort was made shortly thereafter with a committee that
now included five senior executives and five big plebes. This
group added two more tables, completing the first regulatory
documentation in corporate history—the Twelve Tables, which
is perhaps not as elegant a number as ten, but there you have
it. With their genius for public pomp and circumstance and
how it functions to create community, they hammered the
tables out in gold and silver and put them on display so everyone could see them.

As this was going on, most fabulously and instructively for
those attempting a continuing understanding of the executive
mind, the ten great lawmakers who were given the job of dreaming up this republican code of conduct decided, aw, the hell with
it, they would do better running Rome than the Republic and
they would rule as all-powerful dictators instead of duly elected
consuls. So in 449 B.C., the plebes once again were forced to
stage a general strike, brought things to a halt, and engineered a
return to more rational government.

The Twelve Tables are not Hammurabi's Code, powerful and
beautiful in their grandeur and power. They're not even as good
as the lame old Articles of Confederation that the American
founding fathers and mothers hoped would be enough to set our
corporation off on the right foot. They seem kind of weird and
parochial to us now, but who are we to talk? In setting out the
rules of proper conduct for all Romans, the Twelve Tables did a
good job keeping its society at peace with itself far longer than
we've been the peacemakers and nation-builders of the world.

Some highlights of the Twelve Tables. They have a sort of Wild West feel to them, don't they?

- Only legitimate courts could sentence people to death. No freelance executions allowed.
- There were distinctions between forms of murder, depending on the level of intent; punishment for certain forms of murder was often less extreme than that which attended the theft of crops, much as the stealing of a horse in Colorado in 1875 was far more serious than the shooting of an Indian.
- There would be a maximum rate of interest, and a creditor couldn't kill somebody simply because they owed him money. A court would have to recognize the indebtedness, and the debtor would then have thirty days in which to pay, after which he could then be sold into slavery and the price he fetched would be handed over to his creditors.
- Those caught stealing were to be dealt with in two ways. Slaves were flogged and then thrown to their death from a cliff known as the Tarpeian Rock. Freemen were flogged and then forced to repay the person they had stolen from, by working off their debt if necessary.
- Theft of crops was punishable by clubbing to death, which was also the punishment for slandering another citizen.
- In a move to improve public health, no burials were to take place inside city walls.
- Property holders were responsible for the upkeep of the roads that bordered their land.
- Patricians and plebeians were forbidden to marry each other.

- Patricians suffered milder penalties for assaulting another Roman than did plebeians. Assaulting a slave was barely a crime at all.
- It was illegal to have a witch cast spells on anybody, and of course equally forbidden to do so yourself.
- One was permitted to remove a branch from a neighbor's tree which overhung one's property.

In its many antediluvian concerns and rough approach to justice, the Twelve Tables reveal another corporate mind subtly different from our own and yet one that is still very familiar to us. The fact that twenty-five-hundred years ago neighbors were arguing about what to do about that obnoxious tree limb between their property is kind of moving.

United under law, with mechanisms to provide a hearty buy-in to the body of the corporation from all levels of management and employee alike, Rome was ready to move out as one powerful fist to acquire, and then manage with distinction, every other civilized brand that then felt it had a right to its own identity.

At every level of the corporation, there was essential agreement that such domination of all other competitors was not only right and correct, it was inherent in the idea of Rome itself, just as cornering the market on all operating systems was the unquestioned objective of a more recent global empire. Unlike Microsoft, however, there was no power on earth that could be brought to bear to stop it, although they tried, one and all.

Rome during the years of the Republic was united in a pleasant, coherent, militaristic entity that felt it had the right to bring its superior culture and form of governance to whatever alien nation was offensive in its sight. After they conquered, they indulged in an orgy of nation-building, which ended in the locals who were co-opted by Rome running things in its name and reporting back to the mother ship as need be.

There were an incredible panoply of preemptive wars conducted by this united Republic, starting with the ongoing conquest of the Etruscans then moving outward to mastery of all Latium. Beyond the poor Etruscans in Veii there were the hill tribes—the Volscis among them, made most famous by Shakespeare's treatment of Coriolanus, and the Aequians, not to mention an occasional Latin foe from nearby, quite a few of whom decided to hang with Rome rather than depleting their resources and in the end being slaughtered. It's interesting how many times the word "slaughtered" is used in the chronicles of the day. It conveys the message that when Rome was done beating you, they cleaned up loose ends pretty darned well.

As the corporation's rapacious expansionism hit its stride, the propagandists and mythmakers—the best in the business, before or since—kept pushing forth the Roman ideal—the peaceful, industrious citizen soldier, dedicated to his farm and his family.

In 457 B.C., Rome went to crush an Aequian encampment on Mount Algidus. Unfortunately, the Romans marched into a trap and a whole bunch were, that's right, slaughtered by the hill tribe they were trying to wipe out. The survivors hung on to the rocks, waiting for rescue. Enter honest, hardworking, non-career soldier Lucius Quinctius Cincinnatus. Cincinnatus dropped his plow, took up the sword and the powers of dictator, which were granted to all commanders when Rome was under attack, and headed for the hills. In no time, he cut his way through the enemy, creating a corridor through which the entrapped Roman army could escape to fight another day.

Then, embodying the Roman ideal of virtue, Cincinnatus returned to corporate headquarters, put down his powers as dictator, and went back home to feed his chickens. His name was then extolled for ten generations of Romans, and a perfectly fine city in Ohio was named in his honor. Thus did the Republic, in the midst of systematically moving forward to crush the rest of the world, pat itself on the back for its simplicity, humility, and essential peacefulness.

Corporations do this kind of thing for themselves all the time. For instance, some of the companies that view themselves as great forces for ecological sustenance in this world include Exxon, Waste Management, and a host of paper companies that exist to cut down trees.

As the Etruscans faded around 400 B.C. with the fall of their great city of Veii, a serious new foe swarmed in from the north, joined with Rome's enemies on the Italian peninsula, and made a serious pain in the neck of themselves. These were the Gauls, and they handed the corporation a terrible defeat at the Battle of the Allia, almost putting an end to the budding entity then and there.

These Gauls were not the progenitors of the guys who smoked extremely strong cigarettes named in their honor. They were Celts, and a lot closer to Mel Gibson with half his face painted blue. First thing they did was swarm in from the area in central Europe around the Danube and kick around the Etruscans for a while. You have to feel kind of sorry for the Etruscans. They were just playing a different game, much more low-key, less violent, more into the arts and humanities.

Anyhow, these Gauls got into Italy and did a smart thing. There were still a lot of Italians who weren't quite sure they wanted to be Romans. The Gauls basically invited all of those into the action, offering them an opportunity to band together in the kind of numbers that meant something against the big fat bullies, and strike at the heart of the corporate entity to the south.

About thirty thousand Celtic warriors swarmed south. The Roman army met them at the river Allia, which led into the Tiber that fed the corporate headquarters itself.

Underestimating their adversary, the Roman force had only two legions, about ten thousand men, including cavalry. The Romans fought well, but they had never been faced by a force of madmen bent not on acquisition but on total destruction. They were driven into the river, and most fled to Veii in disgrace. The way was open to the city.

When the Celts arrived at the gates of Rome, they found them unguarded. Much of headquarters had been deserted. The only representatives of Rome they found as they made their way around the city, ransacking and pillaging, were the elderly Roman senators sitting in dignified silence in the corporate boardroom. Momentarily flummoxed, the invaders withdrew and thought about things for a while. Then they returned to the Senate, killed whoever was around, and went about their business, not taking over anything, simply stripping all that was of value in their path.

This did not incapacitate Rome, of course. It would have been much worse if the victors had been interested in any management function. The gold, silver, and household appliances might have been carried off, but the idea of Rome, and the right of its senior management to run operations, was left intact.

While the rest of headquarters was temporarily laid low, the fortified capitol remained unbreached. For seven months, the corporate raid continued. Rome then came up with a thousand pounds of gold and the unfriendly acquisitors went away. What a bunch of dummies. They had the greatest nascent corporate organization in their hands, and all they wanted was a boatload of gold.

It took a hundred years for the corporation to get back to its bad self. On the bright side, the Italian peninsula didn't enjoy being occupied and sacked by the fierce and stupid Celts. The subsidiaries of Rome that had been uncertain of their loyalty to the parent corporation now banded together and drove the bad guys into France. In 380 B.C., the Latin League of independent companies that did business with Rome reconstituted to make itself even more congenial to the parent company, and its biggest non-Roman outpost, Tusculum, joined the party, and all its inhabitants became Roman citizens, with full benefit packages and severance deals.

The company also learned another lesson. From that time forth, Rome maintained a gigantic military force, and never again allowed itself to be on the wrong end of an attack if it could help it. Much as the assault on September 11, 2001, produced a certain form of perpetual watchfulness and aggression in its target, Rome from that time forth determined to maintain an unprecedented level of vigilance, and never to be in the position of responding to, rather than initiating, an act of aggression.

This was perhaps the first but not the last time that a smaller and more nimble corporate entity would go at a behemoth with some success. In the 1990s, a number of Internet firms that were way overvalued as a result of the brain-dead partnership of Wall Street and its servile media, managed to leverage themselves into positions of power against more established companies that should, by all rights, have gobbled them up. Instead, there was a time when now forgotten portals almost controlled nation-states with thousands of times their cash flow.

During the next several decades, there were various attempts by forgotten small-potato operations to withstand the inevitable force of Rome. At any time, they must have been aggravating to the Republic. But the destiny of the state was clear, and the consolidation of the region was inevitable.

The thing about consolidation is that there are often several consolidating powers that, while they may be content to let each other live for a time, must eventually come into conflict. As Churchill and Stalin were content to allow each other to operate within each one's designated sphere of influence, Rome and Carthage were perfectly happy to stay at arm's length as long as there were common enemies to defeat, smaller fry to eat. When the world became too small for coexistence, however, the ultimate battle was waged.

In order for Rome to achieve its vision of itself, there could be no Carthage in the world.

# 4

# Wars, Wars and More Wars

I t's absolutely impossible for us to do justice to the complexity and fascinating ins and outs of all the various Punic and other wars in this limited venue. I give up.

For instance, in addition to the various and sundry Punic Wars, there were a whole bunch of others, including campaigns against nations that don't exist anymore as well as Greece and Spain, and people we don't care about any more than we give a damn about dead companies like TelePrompTer or National Cash Register or Moxie, which made a beverage that used to be very popular.

It's easy to get lost in the continual, sweeping warp and weft of our warlike young company as it thumped the surrounding world and made the kind of history that is exclusively written by the winners. We're not going to do that. I'm not Livy, whose attention span is far superior to mine even though he's been dead a couple of thousand years.

Students of protracted battles for control of market share may, however, enjoy a quick bird's-eye view of the back-and-forth battles that determined the future of the first multinational corporation and positioned it for the kind of growth that made history.

A word, before we start, about the brave adversary who fought against our guys for global market share in the many bloody Punic Wars—the glorious Punes. There weren't any. Carthage was originally a Phoenician colony. The Phoenician name for Carthage was "Poenus," who knows why. This led to the nonsensical designation "Punic" in our language. It's too late to change it now.

There were three Punic Wars that stretched over a hundred years or so. Through them all, Carthage Corp. fought with tremendous courage and determination, won a lot of battles, wreaked tremendous destruction on Rome, Inc., and lost the war because, in some ways, Rome was just too stupid and enamored of itself to say uncle. In the end, the victorious Romans knocked down their enemy's corporate headquarters in North Africa, sent all its employees to the Omaha field office, plowed over its home base, and salted its fields so that nothing would grow there again for ten thousand years.

It's possible the losers knew they would eventually end up on the wrong end of the halberd. In 348 B.C., when it was still a working enterprise with the quaint belief that it could operate in the same world as Rome, the boys in Carthage tried to forge a permanent peace with their competitors and partners in conquest, signing a mutual nonaggression pact and sending them a nice Bundt cake. Rome was allowed to conduct business in Carthage and its ports in Africa, Sicily, and Sardinia, but was forbidden from taking over operations in those areas. As if.

The two corporations politely cooperated with each other while dealing with one of the most dynamic, proactive stupid-heads ever to grab a corner office: the Greek commander Pyrrhus, who lives forever in the annals of history as the chief executive who won battles by losing most of his army. The field they fought on was in Sicily, and the proximity of the two corporate powers divvying up an acquisition target, as friends, set the stage for the first war between the two.

And yet they still tried to stay at arm's length from each other. It's easy to imagine why. You're strong, sure, but so is the other guy. He's kind of on your toes, and wow, you'd be big if you could somehow find a way to merge the two of you, with your guys in control, of course.

After a sequence of events in Sicily and Sardinia that is too complex for anyone with executive ADHD to follow, this détente horseshit became impossible to sustain. Something about the Mamnites and the war with Syracuse, and a bunch of misunderstandings, but in reality what it was was that two huge competitors could not coexist in such a small space as the western Mediterranean, with the major business of both entities being acquisition by force.

The first Punic War took place between 264 and 241 B.C. That's twenty-three years. Human beings at the beginning of the twenty-first century have no frame of reference to understand a cultural clash like it. True, things moved more slowly in those days, including both news of the outcome of battles and the strategic reactions to conflicts as they took place. It is not uncommon to hear of executives at headquarters in Rome worrying about a gang of bad guys headed for town, estimated to arrive six months hence. While this is not the way we fight wars now, it is not dissimilar to the way corporate planners wrestle with out-year scenarios in which tiny competitors gain ascendancy ten, fifteen, even twenty years down the road. In my business, there are people who worry that the cell phone may one day replace all current modes of entertainment. Their reaction to this problem, as it was in Rome, is to posit a succession of acquisitions by which the future competition may one day be subsumed into the corporate body. In other words, if you can't beat them, buy them. And if you can't buy them, crush them.

In the first three years of the first Punic War, the early 260s, our guys captured the number two business center in Sicily after the mighty Syracuse—Acragas, which they rebranded, not very creatively, as Agrigentum. This made things tough for Carthage in any land-based battle, but had the salutary effect, for them, of forcing them to rely on their navy, which was very powerful and developed, unlike that of Rome, which didn't even have a major port to call its own yet. A technology gap needed to be addressed. Rome, Inc. solved this problem the same way Japan, Inc. became a competitor to USA Corp.—by imitating that which it had not yet created.

But that wasn't all Rome did. They employed scientists and inventors—I'm betting the best of them were Greek and Phoenician slaves—and changed the game entirely by creating a new way of fighting on the water. The way the prephilanthropic Michael Milken ushered in the decade of greed with the powerful weapon known as the junk bond, the first multinational corporation cooked up a series of grapples and metal planks that incapacitated an enemy ship, made it easy to immobilize and then board. At that point, the Roman fighter was then on much more familiar turf, standing on solid ground and ready to go about the business he knew best—slashing, stabbing, and, of course, hacking.

In 256 B.C., in this manner, Rome destroyed the best part of Carthage's fleet, then pursued their enemy back to their home base in Africa, where they failed to press their advantage successfully. There was more fighting, which was inconclusive, and the Romans sailed back for home. The two sides had fought each other to a standstill. The operations in Sicily were 90 percent settled in Rome's column, but there were still some pesky Punic outposts that refused to be taken. For some reason, the other guys continued to believe they had a right to do business in the same general marketplace as their biggest competitor. So they once again tried to make peace. But Rome wasn't after peace. It was after market share and the humiliation of its enemies.

Honor. Courage. A willingness to give one's life for the corporation. These are the values that fueled double-digit growth in those formative years for our developing corporate state. Take Regulus. A Roman consul, he was captured by Carthage in the first, unsuccessful African campaign, and was rotting somewhere in the executive departure lounge of Punic HQ. The senior management of the enemy came to him and offered him a proposition. Go home, they said. Give your word as a Roman that you will sue for peace in our behalf and you will have your freedom. If you fail, give your word as a Roman that you will return and we will kill you in a way we haven't determined yet, but we're working on it. Okay, says Regulus. So he goes back to Rome and, without a thought for his own personal situation, tells the Senate that the other guys want peace, don't listen to them, rededicate yourselves to stamping those bastards out. The Senate thanks him, agrees with him, and sends him back to Carthage to deliver the rotten news that the competitive battle for dominance of the known world will continue. Regulus, who could have thumbed his nose at his North African hosts and sent a polite Dear Guys letter, mounts up, goes back to Carthage with the really bad news, and is forthwith torn to shreds by his disappointed captors.

Sometime later Carthage begins to produce leaders from the Barca family, an enormously resilient, stubborn, violent, and gifted group of senior executives with entertaining names who really gave Rome a run for its money over many, many years. The first is Hamilcar, who took over the war in 247 B.C., built new ports in western Sicily from which he could raid Roman enclaves with impunity. This annoyed our board of directors, which sucked it up, put out a call for private donations, and built a new navy (the old one had been destroyed in a storm) to kick Hamilcar back to Africa.

Defeated, Hamilcar then had to subdue the very large and hostile remnant of the army he had raised to fight Rome before it all came undone. These tough, truculent mercenaries had not been paid and had loyalty to no one. This, in the end, over a period of a hundred years, became perhaps the greatest problem for Carthage, the factor that ultimately doomed them to defeat. Rome relied for its expansion and defense on an army of citizen soldiers—full-time employees of the corporation. Carthage relied on mercenaries—per diem employees and consultants. Any enterprise that must depend on those types of workers is at a significant disadvantage when fighting against a troop that gets full benefits and a modest but sustainable retirement package.

Carthage was left with Spain to defend and sculpt into a halfway decent market for its operations. Spain was tough. It was full of mean, ornery locals, and teeming with Greek and Roman development guys looking into their own possibilities in the region. Enter the next Barca—Hasdrubal the Elder, who does so well in the development of new Iberian product lines that Rome decides to let him live, establishing a line of demarcation between their business interests and Carthage's in the region in 226 B.C. In the next few years, the entire sales territory south of the Ebro River was Carthage's, with only one small local operation in that area sympathetic to Roman interests.

After Hasdrubal is murdered by a nasty competitor, he is succeeded as senior vice president in charge of Spanish operations by the most famous Barca of them all, Hannibal, the son of Hamilcar. When Hannibal was a child, he was forced to make a vow to hate all Romans for the rest of his life. He lived up to that oath and caused the corporation a great deal of trouble before he was laid to rest.

Hannibal is one of those action-oriented executives loved by the troops. He carries with him the Big Idea of Carthage—which is to avenge the indignities of the past and kick Rome upside its arrogant, expansionist head.

While Rome is distracted with military engagements elsewhere, Hannibal gets very aggressive. First he attacks the one

Roman client within his territory, the town of Saguntum, and, while Rome is attempting to deal with this problem diplomatically, takes the city. The second Punic War is begun, Carthage dragged into it by the aggression, egomania, and determination of its own military commander. This won't be the last time a charismatic vision guy wreaks a world of hurt on friends and enemies alike. In all businesses, including the military and government, the line between vision and madness is sometimes ill defined. The vision thing is fun for a while, then the organization suffers.

Hannibal Barca was one of the great out-of-the-box thinkers and strategic planners, and he didn't give up until he lost the support of his own senior management—and, of course, a lot of lives along the way. Hannibal's idea was to tie up Rome in Africa and then, with the help of the many little mom-and-pop operations that hated Rome in the south of France and northern Italy, invade the boot itself and set up shop right on Rome's doorstep, frightening the toga boys and eventually piercing the heart of the great corporation in its own hometown. How to get there? By the hardest way possible—over the Alps. In winter. Just exactly what any sane manager would never think of doing. And while we're at it, let's bring along something no Roman, no Italian has ever seen before: elephants. Big, scary, weird elephants. That ought to rock their world, huh?

Hannibal entered Italy expecting two things: (1) support of the locals, who had been acquired by Roman force, and (2) support of his own senior management back in Carthage—in the form of troops. He found neither. The power of the dominant culture, and Rome's strategy of making its subjects into citizens, had stripped the Italian peninsula of substantial forces who had a bone to pick with their executive cadre. And Carthage? They considered this Hannibal maniac a total hotdog, a dangerous and uncontrollable player, a threat to the future security of the entity. And they were right.

So Hannibal takes up residence in Italy, from whence he can make trouble in Syracuse and in Macedon, but he's not really going anywhere. He's working. He's in business. But the long-term scenario doesn't look so good. He's a brilliant man of action—but sometimes the business environment doesn't call for such men. TWA did fine with Howard Hughes when it was a start-up that needed energy and inspiration. Later, when it was a true business, it required guys in suits, not some crazy nutbag with six-inch fingernails.

The war continues. Rome has mastered the strategy of many a divorce attorney—Fabian tactics, where you just do nothing until the adversary gets so sick of the conflict they accede to your demands. And still Hannibal fights on, in many many interesting campaigns and battles you won't be hearing about here. Throughout, he suffers from an almost complete lack of reinforcements coming from his own corporate headquarters in Africa. Realizing his own guys aren't in his corner, Hannibal sends for his brother, Hasdrubal the Younger, who comes all the way from Spain to get killed before being able to help.

In the meantime, the great Roman executive Scipio uses Hannibal's inattention to business in Spain to kick all Carthage interests out of there. Careful to build alliances that support the overall effort, Rome also shores up its friendships with the

Numidians in Africa. This will come in handy later. You can't have too many friends.

In 202 B.C., Hannibal and his brother, Mago, who had somehow escaped the letter *H,* are called back to defend headquarters in Africa from the destruction he had called down on it. At Zama, Scipio meets the last ragtag schnooks in a Punic uniform and the war is won for the good guys. Terms are very severe:

- Carthage out of Spain.
- All field offices in Africa are closed.
- No acquisition or expansion without Roman permission, and don't hold your breath.
- Carthage permitted to keep ten ships, that's all. All the rest are surrendered to Rome. We'll take the elephants, too, by the way. They're cool.
- Now let's talk about money—ten thousand talents over a period of fifty years. That's right, you're working for us now.
- If you try to fight us again, we will bury you.

Hannibal sticks around Carthage for a while, but things are no good for him there. There's nothing left to buy or build. And he's not a corporate guy. He's an operator. He gets out of town and heads for a place that's willing to hire him on a consulting basis to be a continuing pain in the ass to Rome.

Rome! It's what's happening. Bold and now within striking distance of control not only of Italy but maybe even of Greece, Spain, Macedon, Gaul! The notion of a true multinational corporation is taking shape, with some more unfriendly acquisitions:

Philip V of Macedon seems to think he can move in on little operations in Greece here and there and turn them into a line extension of his existing stuff. Rome joins with all of them, plays the role of the good guy, and in the end they know which side it's smart to be on. Because when Philip takes over an operation, he's like an executive from Disney, IBM, or General Electric, replacing even the most talented local senior management with his own cronies. Rome, on the other hand, always follows an acquisition, even an unfriendly one, with an outstretched hand and lots of goodies for existing middle management. Roman citizenship, continued power, the dignity of a Roman title on your business card; what could be bad? Philip is defeated in a decisive battle in a place whose name you don't need to know because you'll forget it five minutes later anyhow. The point is, our guys are doing very well in Greece and have neutralized yet another senior management structure that thought it was in competition with us.

Anti-Roman elements in Greece now align with Antiochus of Syria, famous for all students of Jewish holidays as a very bad guy. Guess who's helping him out? Hannibal! You've got to say the guy had excellent powers of concentration. I guess that's what happens when you swear an eternal hatred for something as a child. I know adults who to this day won't eat liver. As a complete antithesis of this emotionalism, there is the fact that for the engagement against Syria, Rome aligns itself with its former blood enemy, Philip of Macedon, proving that great corporations are opportunistic and not sticklers about doing what's necessary when the time comes, no matter who it might be necessary with.

Rome tracks Antiochus down near the city of Magnesia, the first time the company does business in the growing Asia territory. Things don't go well for the Syrian army, and they lose more than fifty thousand men, while, legend has it, the Romans lose less than five hundred. Subsequent observers express disbelief at this discrepancy. They have clearly never been on the wrong side of a merger of equals. Once again, Rome gets the elephants, a lot of money, and all the territories of the obnoxious Syrians, which they distribute to their allies in the fight.

We're now well after 200 B.C., and getting relatively close to the end of the Republic, which, you will note, has constantly been at war throughout its life as it conducted all its other businesses.

If you're getting tired of hearing about all these wars, imagine how it felt to be a Roman citizen, expected to serve and die continually, even if you were doing very well with the fur trade, say, or just felt like sitting around and drinking wine. That's why the idea of the corporation becomes so essential. No grand idea to get the troops out of their Barcaloungers means no soldiers to build the nation-state.

There are further wars in what is now southern France, Spain, Greece, and Macedonia, lots of interesting battles I'm sure you'll want to read about elsewhere.

Meanwhile, back in northern Africa, pesky, brave Carthage just won't stay down! Amazing dudes. The powers that be there, they just want to do business now. They're good at it. And they want to be friends with Rome and not waste their resources in constant destructive wrangling with the big dog around the corner.

Carthage really doesn't have a chance. Then as now, it was tough to be a contained, well-focused enterprise in an era of mass consolidation. Just try being a small ad agency these days. To its south, Carthage faced the Numidians, friends of Rome, who kept pick-pick-picking away at their trade routes. Carthage appealed to Rome, because it had to, by treaty, to conduct any defensive activity whatsoever. Rome sent an emissary to look into the situation—Marcus Cato, who was fond of ending his speeches, no matter what they were about, with the words "Destroy Carthage!" He found in favor of the Numidians.

Backs to the wall, their remaining business operations in jeopardy, Carthage fought the Numidians, staying well clear of their powerful rulers on the Tiber. It did them no good. The Senate had had enough of this annoying competitive culture. There could be only one sheriff in town.

Rome dispatched a large army to pay a visit to Carthage, eighty thousand infantry and four thousand horse. Their orders were not to beat the other side, but to annihilate it entirely. For two years, the Romans besieged Carthage, giving it significant time to get organized while its own soldiers got sick in the swamps. Scipio, who was later to take the surname Africanus in honor of his success, came over from Rome, and, after taking a little time to get things together, occupied the outskirts of town, closed the harbor to starve his enemies, then hit the city hard, breaking through the gates without too much trouble and then going from house to house for about a week, slaughtering. The city was then burned, its fifty thousand survivors sold into slavery, and the fields around it rendered poisonous to any living thing. Scipio was honored and eventually became consul due to his great military leadership and the fact that there were still plenty of wars to fight going forward. It was 146 B.C.

Oh so many wars! These were not disruptions in the business of the corporation—they *were* the business of the corporation, the first step in any strategic plan then extant. There were wars against slaves, which ended, in Sicily, with more than twenty thousand crucifixions, and wars against Spain and so forth, but by about 100 B.C. the shape of the business world was clear: it was Rome's world, everybody else had to live in it.

# 5

# Crazy Republicans

W hat we have, then, as we get about a hundred years before the birth of Christ, is the first known society to produce the nexus of hypermilitary activity, industrialism, and political power known since Ike coined the term, in his farewell address in 1959, as the military-industrial complex.

The control of such nation-states is put in the hands of those who maintain a role in all of these three elements, with a completely permeable barrier between all three.

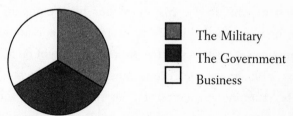

The Military
The Government
Business

Those who labor in any one of the three areas may pursue their careers in any of the other two. It takes a certain kind of executive to pull that off.

When I worked for a large multinational corporation that no longer exists, our board of directors was stocked with former officials of the Nixon administration. They helped us understand by which criteria the government selected electronic guidance systems for missiles and the maintenance contracts of nuclear reactors both domestic and military, including submarines.

This elegant synergy was invented in Rome—for nowhere before or since did a corporation create such well-rounded Renaissance men; this at least a thousand years before the actual Renaissance. It may not be completely coincidental that the next time such individuals appeared, it was in Rome, unless you count Tuscany, which also belonged to Rome.

Up until this point—about 100 B.C.—there were great generals, and great statesmen, and great businesspeople, and sometimes there were individuals who combined one or two of these capabilities into a killer package.

But suddenly, with the consolidation of the area around Italy itself, and the conquest of its major competition—Greek, Macedonian, Etruscan, and, most importantly, Carthaginian— we reach a point in the history of our little company where greater men were called for if the strategy of precipitous growth by aggressive acquisition was to continue. And right on schedule, it seems, a phalanx of such extraordinary men was created; larger than life, stunning in their power, determination, and the scope of their talents. Men who combined military prowess with business acumen and political subtlety, too. Some of them could even write poetry.

Why were these men needed? Why couldn't this beautiful, elegant, midsize corporate entity, going gangbusters, simply settle down, tend its fields and its new colonies the way its supposed heroes of ancient days like Cincinnatus had done, pull back from its destiny, and simply allow the rest of the world, and its own male population (which must have been sick of all the hacking and slashing, at least of *them*), to live in peace and security?

The strategic problem for the corporation was that there was no peace without continual war. The marketplace in which it operated, from Scotland to India and even up to Mongolia, was marked by a global fluidity and lack of meaningful national boundaries that made a culture's survival dependent on knocking out the other guy before he got the jump on you. There were no laws but power. The land teemed with Aryans and Gauls and Mongols and Celts and Picts and Persians and Egyptians, all of them looking for properties to trade with, merge with, and acquire by force if necessary. Pond scum like the Vandals, or their ancestors at this time, favored simply showing up, killing everybody, trashing the entire place, raping the women, slaughtering the children. There was a lot at stake. Those who were acquired or simply trashed for profit lost not only their houses in Malibu, Grosse Pointe, or Sag Harbor. They lost their lunch, or what was left of it.

It isn't that Rome minded the never-ending struggle. They liked their game and the way they played it. But there was never any question in the corporate consciousness that the alternative to acquisition and colonization of places like Gaul, Egypt, and Mesopotamia was not peace but loss of market share in the region and the eventual unfriendly takeover of their own field operations.

The problem was what this incessant, bloody warfare and its implications on future strategies had done to the executive mind. You had to be nuts to be a success at that juncture. Think about it. To be a functional senior manager in this culture you had to be capable of . . .

- Killing and enslaving entire populations of previously functional smaller entities
- Crucifying your foes in large numbers
- Making deals with colleagues you had every intention of killing later
- Marrying and divorcing women for political reasons
- Lusting for positions you had every reason to believe would end in your suicide or violent death, probably soon
- Spending an enormous amount of time on the road in places that make Schenectady look like Rome
- Imagining yourself governor of Egypt or Syria or some equally old and impressive civilization that by any reasonable standard you had no right to rule and certainly knew very little about
- Commissioning the erecting of statues of yourself

That's just for starters.

Before 100 B.C., the incidence of gigantic, pathological, preening, egotistical and thoroughly modern nutcases in the ranks of senior management is relatively rare, and you have many examples of noble Romans who lived to serve the state. After, you begin to get moguls. In the absence of a strong center, and the corruption of daily life in the Republic, these competing moguls have free rein to marshal their forces and make a run at the top slot, which they may occupy for a time, but never own.

There are also several other factors at work here that make the whole situation at the end of the Republic creepily evocative of our own situation. Perhaps most striking is the fact that as the Roman Republic wound down, there developed for the first time a stark, murderous hatred between the left and right wings of the culture.

On the Right, there was a corrupt and entrenched Senate, jealous of its powers and perks, willing to do anything to maintain the status quo. These were the patricians, who were known at that point for some reason we don't care about as the *optimates*. On what might pass for the Left, there were men of the people, those who had attained their power and wealth not by inheritance but by the sweat of their own brows and the blood of their sons and ancestors. These were the *populares*.

It's important to keep in mind that both classes—Left and Right—were members of the ruling class. But on the Left, unlike now, there was a constant awareness of the importance of the mob, which gave it some of the power now enjoyed by our own Republicans.

Neither optimates nor populares were very nice guys. But when it came to corruption, greed, and underhandedness, you had to hand it to those sneaky togas in the Senate. They bribed people, stole elections, ran the government to enhance their business interests, and, like all Romans, were pretty comfortable killing people. On the other hand, the populares would later be known for slaughtering everybody who opposed them, including, of course, the requisite murders of countless slaves and children. As governors of the field operations, they routinely stole the coins from the eyes of the dead. So it's hard to pick a white horse here.

As we march down the path toward the end of the Republic and the rise of the empire—which was a big improvement over the nutty, disorganized corporate bureaucracy, teeming with backstabbers and suck-ups—we will see each mogul attach himself to one party or another, mostly for opportunistic reasons. There are no idealists here, except, perhaps, for crazy reactionaries like Cicero and Cato, who would rather die than see the end of the fictional state that existed only in their minds, and Julius Caesar, who embodied all that was extraordinary in the Roman executive character, and was killed for it by a bunch of weasels.

This was a battle between the haves and the have-mores, not a struggle between the rich and the poor. But the poor knew what side they were on—the Left—although they were always willing to talk.

What is most interesting to us, as we home in on this critical period of about a hundred years, is the development of the kind of boss we recognize, in perhaps a much more outsized and primitive form, but perhaps not. We aren't permitted to do the things these Roman moguls did as part of their portfolio, but the characteristics of each is powerfully familiar to us.

There were quite a few of them, these crazy republicans. The intriguing thing is that they generally came in twos—pairs of engorged, self-centered madmen whose insanity fit so well with the prevailing needs of the culture that it was interpreted as greatness. And perhaps it was.

All of these men were monsters. All of them were interesting. But Marius, Caius Marius, represents most purely all that was fascinating, deplorable, and admirable about Rome. You may recognize him if you work for a company that's big enough and important enough to generate a seriously delusional senior executive.

# 6

# Marius, the First Mogul

Caius Marius was born to parents who had nothing and who were nobody. From start to finish, he was the quintessential self-made man. In the ancient world, that was an amazing thing, and only Rome, Inc., up to that point in history, could have created the climate of entrepreneurial opportunity in which a poor little ragamuffin from the stinky slums of the city could rise to be consul—the highest position in the land!—more times than any other Roman in the history of the Republic. Okay, he didn't deserve the job a couple of times, and he sort of stole it once or twice, but that's pretty impressive, too, right?

Marius was a crazy, juiced-up, bombastically angry mother, and he wouldn't stay down, no matter what. There was a statue of the man himself at Ravenna, a small, lovely northern Italian town which, sadly, became the corporate center for a while when the wheezing, overextended organization was on its last legs and Rome was in ruin. The statue was "quite corresponding with that roughness and harshness of character that is ascribed to him,"

Plutarch wrote. "Being naturally valiant and warlike, and more acquainted also with the discipline of the camp than of the city, he could not moderate his passion when in authority." I don't know about you, but that gives me a nice frisson of recognition.

He was rude, too. One time, at a celebration of one of his great triumphs, he came and immediately departed, showing no interest in the performance because it was in Greek, a language he never took the trouble to learn, partially because it was often taught by slaves upon whom he looked down. In fact, the historian notes, he could have done with a couple of Greek graces, or he might have never "brought his incomparable actions, both in war and peace, to so unworthy a conclusion, or wrecked himself, so to say, upon an old age of cruelty and vindictiveness, through passion, ill-timed ambition, and insatiable cupidity." Passion. Ill-timed ambition. Insatiable cupidity. Makes you feel kind of at home, doesn't it?

Marius was raised in a little cow town well outside of Rome— rude and undeveloped, but brimming with those mythic Roman virtues of simplicity, hard work, and family life. He joined the corporation very young, as a soldier, which is analogous in contemporary terms, I think, to coming in through the Sales Department. Most senior officers now collecting eight- and nine-figure salaries came to their companies through that door. Salespeople fight every day, and are judged by what they have done for the firm lately, not over a period of time. They have to work drunk, and they don't punch a time clock. They live and die by maintaining the territory that is given to them, and conquering more. They are also highly personable, insincere when they need to be, and vicious in a close fight. All these qualities lead to a certain kind of combative, results-oriented personality that suits itself to senior management very nicely.

Marius began his working life as a foot soldier fighting for Scipio Africanus, who you will remember was instrumental in turning Carthage into a parking lot. After that, he besieged Numantia, which is just south of another place that no longer exists in Africa. In this campaign, which was one of perhaps a dozen that were going on in the Hacking and Slashing Department at that time, Marius proved himself to be the bravest of his contemporaries, and came to the notice of the senior vice president of field operations, Scipio himself. He was particularly adept in bringing the army, which was sinking into luxury and excess, into some kind of order. This, too, is refreshingly familiar to us. How many senior officers do you know who earned the affection of ultrasenior management by cutting costs and keeping a hard eye on the expenses of the foot soldiers?

In a truly fortunate stroke for the young mogul-to-be, his boss saw him actually kill a man in hand-to-hand combat. Later, at a party, as his betters sucked up the free scotch and wolfed down the pigs in a blanket and teeny quesadillas, the subject arose, in that great corporate atmosphere of macho drunkenness and swaggering power, of who might be fit to succeed Scipio himself, at which point the old man clapped Young Marius on the shoulder and said, "Hey! Why not my man Marius here?" At that moment, Marius saw his future, and it was not simply the future of a sales weasel. From that time forth he had his eye on the kind of office that has its own bathroom and two assistants in the ante-chamber outside.

Coming back from his initial gig, full of pith and vinegar, with an ego the size of his ambition, Marius threw himself into politics. Through family connections, he had himself named a tribune of the people, a post that derived its power directly from the amount of kissing up you did to the common corporate employee. He immediately introduced a piece of legislation that would have limited the power of the big noises that ran the judiciary, for Marius's self-interest lay in casting his lot with the people, which in that day made him a man of the Left.

This did not sit well with Cotta, the senior officer at the time, who got the Senate to attack Marius for proposing it. This was no light thing back then. People who annoyed others in politics often found themselves in prison, or even running down the street with their sheets flying, an armed mob hired by one partisan or another screaming behind them for blood. Gangs were routinely hired by one senator or another to off an obnoxious adversary, especially one who was not a patrician.

But was our Marius worried? Was he scared? Did he scurry around behind the scenes trying to get this little problem with his superiors, who were older and presumably more honed in statecraft, solved? Most importantly, did he back off his legislation? Okay, those are all rhetorical questions. Of course he didn't.

What he did was this: he marched into the Senate, which was far more impressive than any boardroom any of us have ever been in, and told Cotta that if he didn't back off he would have him thrown into prison.

Chutzpah! What is it?

It is, in fact, the Chutzpah Factor that differentiates the mogul from his more quotidian managerial counterpart in the business cosmology. It may be defined by those who need a definition as "nerve," but is so much more than that, adding a component of arrogance and irrationality to the basic ingredients of bravery and daring.

Let's look at a few moguls through the ages and the kinds of chutzpah that helped them get where they were in their day.

### Acts of Mogulian Chutzpah

| MOGUL | ACT OF CHUTZPAH |
|---|---|
| Walt Disney | Purchased huge chunk of Florida for grandiose theme park |
| Bill Gates | Tried to corner the browser market by squashing competition |
| Bob Pittman | Took over Time Warner |
| Jerry Levin | Allowed Bob Pittman to take over Time Warner |
| Barry Diller | Announced "acquisition" of CBS before checking with his boss and banker, Brian Roberts |
| Brian Roberts | Told Barry Diller he couldn't have CBS to play with |
| Martha Stewart | Lied to SEC |
| Jack Welch | Charged GE for greens fees |
| Donald Trump | Hair |

Now back to the Senate, where Marius has just threatened to throw the current chairman of the board into prison. Having left Cotta dumbfounded, Marius turned to Metellus, another important suit, and, after ascertaining that Metellus, too, was against him, called security and had Metellus clapped into chains. The Senate complied shortly thereafter, and passed the new, populist law, whatever it was.

Marius had won, and exited the Senate to the cheers of the mob outside, who recognized a guy who could get things done for It.

The crucial point in this story is that this pischer, this minor-league foot soldier, a bullethead who came from nothing, who had a good but not particularly famous record in some territorial operation someplace, faced down a roomful of men who could command the best table in any restaurant they entered. It is crazy people who believe in themselves to this extent, who form the core of all truly successful senior management.

It is also important to note that Marius did not come in and separate his bosses' heads from their chubby shoulders. No, he was working within the system but *dominating it with his personality,* just as our own swaggering moguls do to this day as long as they can get away with it. Think of how many people told Dave Thomas that there were better choices than he to do the on-air spots for Wendy's. He just told them to stuff it. He ran the place. He was going to do the spots. Anybody disagree? No? That's settled, then.

Right after he won the love of the Left, by the way, Marius sided with the Senate in a debate over the distribution of corn, and won the admiration of the Right, demonstrating yet another great mogul trait: intelligent opportunism, as differentiated from the stupid kind.

After his great success in the role of tribune, Marius, once again living the legend in his own mind, ran for another office and stumbled. When it was clear he wasn't getting that slot, he opted to go after something smaller, but came across just a little too hot and lost that one too. At that point, almost out of the good stuff completely, he bribed his way into a praetorship, in so doing demonstrating his tendency, also common among slightly demented senior management, for getting himself into trouble. There was a trial in which he was accused of the crime of greasing his way into the position. For a while it went badly, and then he was acquitted, thus providing evidence of the subsequent and equally compelling truth that no matter how much trouble moguls get themselves into, they generally come out smelling like a rose in the end. This is because, as many talents and abilities as they possess, they cannot envision themselves losing, even when they have lost. And so they do not, even when they do.

Marius wasn't a particularly good praetor. He made a decent showing by clearing some robbers out of Spain, which at that time, according to at least one historian, still viewed thieving as a reputable occupation. He wasn't rich and he wasn't particularly well-spoken, either, which was the way Romans generally distinguished themselves and gained power in those days. But his simple way of living and willingness to work hard got him places.

And although he wasn't particularly smooth or good-looking,

there must have been something prepossessing about him, because he made a terrific match when it came time for him to take a wife. This turned out, in an uncommon stroke of luck, to be Julia, the aunt of the man who was to become the greatest Roman of them all, Julius Caesar, who later stated that he was deeply influenced by this earlier iteration of senior manager.

Not long after, there was a big war in Africa against a tribal leader named Jugurtha. The Jugurthine war was a vicious, tough campaign, and the outcome was by no means certain. Metellus, who was consul at that time, brought Marius along as one of his lieutenants, for while the kid was obnoxious as a politician, he was a hell of a fighter. While Hotshot was there, he did not, like other subordinates, labor in the shadow of his boss, ascribing his success to his position in the power structure, but rather viewed his achievements as a direct product of Fortune itself. In the field, he performed with great bravery—and no job was too large or too small. He lived and fought with the common soldiers, stayed sober (unlike many in the executive branch), and kept clear of his management peers. Plutarch points out:

> It is the most obliging sight in the world to the Roman soldier to see a commander eat the same bread as himself, or lie upon an ordinary bed, or assist the work in drawing a trench and raising a bulwark. For they do not so much admire those that confer honors and riches upon them, as those that partake of the same labor and danger with themselves; but love them better that will vouchsafe to join in their work, than those that encourage their idleness.

So Marius became famous in the way that a George S. Patton embodied the spirit of every American ground soldier during the Second World War. And there were those who wrote home from the front saying that Jugurtha would never be destroyed unless Marius took over as consul. This understandably upset his boss.

There was another beef between them as well. In a side campaign at the midsize town of Vaga worked a friend of Consul Metellus, a fellow named Turpillius. He was a pretty good guy, he treated the locals kindly and fairly, and for that reason fell into the hands of the enemy, who took the city and released him, possibly because they had nothing against him, because he was so ineffectual. Marius, being one of those in the decision-making committee, was very large on the need to punish the consul's friend, and so, as a consequence, Turpillius was put to death for treason. He was later cleared, and Metellus was very upset. Marius, on the other hand, was not, letting it be known that he was the prime mover in the decision to execute the boss's best friend.

Now our ambitious, ruthless hero was ready to go back to headquarters and stand for his boss's job. And that is exactly what he did. His fame was established and new. People, then as now, like a new public toy to play with. There was also a sense of something exceptional that voters always like—a man of action, with ambition so huge and character so large that it was a come-on to the spirit that moved the city itself. To any Roman immersed in the corporate culture at that time, this tough, pug-ugly, driven executive was everything Rome envisioned as its true self.

So Marius was elected to the highest post in the land for the first of seven times, and immediately began allowing all kinds of riffraff into the army. Up until that point, a man had to have property and standing to fight against Rome's enemies. Now even slaves and the poor could get in. He carried his generally left-wing stance to a higher level yet, making arrogant speeches about how he had won the consul post because the aristocracy was a bunch of sissies, statements not unlike those recently uttered by that great populist hero of California, the Governator himself, Arnold Schwarzenegger.

So Marius went to Africa and took over his old boss's army and wrested all the credit he could from winning the war even though it was Metellus who had actually accomplished that task. All that remained was the apprehension of Jugurtha himself.

Then something very interesting happened, a little glitch in Marius's script that was an augury of things to come. Just as he was about to nab the headlines as the big winner of the war, a younger executive, Sulla, got his hands on the unfortunate Jugurtha via a complicated series of backstage shenanigans, and ended up with a fair share of the fame Marius sought for his own greedy self. There were even statues and coins commemorating the moment when Sulla took possession of the enemy! Grating! Galling! Horribly aggravating!

As we've already noticed, each mogul in history, except perhaps Warren Buffett, has his antimogul, the one who flies in his face and wrecks his perfect self-mythology:

| MOGUL | ANTIMOGUL |
|-------|-----------|
| Marius | Sulla |
| Pompey | Caesar |
| Antony | Octavian |
| Howard Hughes | Howard Hughes |
| Hugh Hefner | Larry Flynt |
| Rupert Murdoch | Lachlan Murdoch |
| Bill Gates | Steve Jobs |
| Michael Eisner | Michael Ovitz/Jeffrey Katzenberg/Roy Disney/etc. |

Throughout his life, as many accomplishments as he achieved, Marius battled against Sulla, and it's tough, in the end, to perceive who won, since both turned into monsters before too long, as we will see. For some reason I find myself rooting for Marius in each setback and trial, while Sulla, for his part, makes me nervous, the same way I often get a kick out of grand, gross masters of excess like Dennis Kozlowski, while having nothing but a low-level annoyed contempt for self-serving greedmeisters like Enron's senior management, Kenny Boy Lay in particular, and outright fear of some moguls now extant, to the point where I will not even utter their names. You know who they are.

As the years went by, people hated Marius and loved Marius, he had his supporters on the Left in the lower house and the mob, and his detractors on the Right and in the Center, particularly those whose families he killed or whom he insulted in pub-

lic. But each time a serious business crisis hit the corporation—
and that happened with alarming regularity, as we know—the
populace shed its internecine differences and turned to the most
direct, least conflicted, most accomplished field executive it possessed. And that's how Marius became consul seven times—by
being the biggest ass-kicker in a corporation where ass-kicking
was Job One.

You will remember that in his climb over everything in his
path, Marius supplanted his old boss, Metellus. After ascertaining that it was probably a bad idea to kill such a noted senior officer, Marius worked ceaselessly through his contacts on the board
to have Metellus sent to the field office in Petaluma. When time
passed and Metellus's friends succeeded in having him called
back to corporate headquarters, essentially to die, since he was
quite old by that time, Marius got so pissed off that he scheduled
a long vacation in Hilton Head rather than be in Rome when
Metellus returned.

Anyhow, there were a lot of wars during the old boy's seven
terms as consul. Of particular interest are the many ways he con-
nived to keep his post as the nation's number one military and
political commander, even going so far as to buy the post at least
once. He defeated the Teutons and the Cimbri and a lot of other
unwashed, ugly dudes, and Rome grew, as it always did in those
days, and Marius was unchallenged in glory and the number of
people who justifiably feared him.

Sulla was equally vicious, smart and dynamic, just as ugly, if
not more so, and, unlike Marius, was convinced of his own
propensity for good luck. In fact, he named himself Sulla Felix,

which may be translated as Sulla the Lucky Guy. Whatever delusions our friend Marius entertained, the idea that he was inherently fortunate was not one of them, which was why he constantly conspired against all comers in a generally paranoid fog.

Marius, now aging, increasingly found himself in the role of bystander in the acquisition business, and generally felt rotten about things, and increasingly exposed as others reaped the glories. This might have been the kind of funk guys fall into when their enemies do well in any business, like when Katzenberg sees a Disney cartoon at number one for a week or two, except for the fact that Marius was such a huge pain in the ass when he was in power that his enemies truly feared what he would be like when he was forced out of it. A lion in winter is one thing. A *Tyrannosaurus rex* is another.

Which brings us to the last days of this first mogul. For a while, at the beginning of the end, Marius hung in there and continued to fight the enemies of Rome, and of himself, but his body was beginning to desert him. He had always prided himself on his ability to kick butt, hand to hand. Now he had to be a little more clever. When one enemy called out on the field of battle, "If you are indeed the great Marius, come out and prove it!" he was forced to reply, "Come and make me!" which was deemed clever and wise, but probably not as much fun as riding out and turning the guy's head, as Frank Miller might say, into a PEZ dispenser.

The next big deal on the horizon was the coming war with the Eastern king Mithradates. When the strategic planning for the pending unfriendly acquisition was under way, most sane people thought that Sulla was the right guy for the job. But there were those like Sulpicius, the tribune of the people, who suggested Marius, for mostly political reasons. Public opinion was divided, but most intelligent people saw some obvious problems.

First, the guy was *old*. There were those who jeered at Marius, told him to forget about the battles ahead and go to the baths at Baiae, where he could take care of his body, which was worn out and covered with catarrhs, whatever those might be.

He had also, like many, many moguls before and since, gotten soft in the head, heart, and stomach, and too fond of his opulent digs at Misenum, which were "more effeminately and luxuriously furnished than seemed to become one that had seen service in so many and great wars and expeditions." There follows in Plutarch an interesting discussion of property values at the time, with a discussion of how the price of villas had appreciated around those parts in just a few years' time, that reads like it could have been written in last week's *New York Observer*. That's the milieu fighting moguls find themselves immersed in when they reach a certain stage of their careers. In my experience, when an executive starts talking about the wonders of his get-away spot in Palm Beach, Malibu, or the Hamptons, I know he's ready for the slag heap.

Not that they don't fight it. In a move so reminiscent to me of several geriatric moguls I have known that it brings tiny tears of appreciation to my eye, it is said that Marius, ancient by the standards of his day, creaky from a life of battle, fat and way past it, still went down to the fields where the young men worked out *every single day* and exercised with the frosty kids, showing he could still hoist himself up on a horse and get the job done, armor and all.

The world found Marius strutting around on the fields of Mars to be pretty ridiculous. But his desire to leave the supreme comfort of his place on Fifth and Fifty-seventh and head off to Cappadocia to fight Mithradates? That was something else again—a dangerous notion that could threaten Rome itself if the egotism and delusional faux youthfulness of the old general was allowed to prevail for political reasons.

He gave it a solid try, though. At that time, as it was some years before, the corporate center was subject to innumerable palace coups, backstabbing weasels assaulting each other in the executive suite, kind of like the way things were at Xerox in the nineties. Sensing weakness at the corporate center, Sulpicius— the guy who pushed for Marius in the first place—attracted some six hundred plebes of the highest order and named them antisenators. With these as his guard, he went into the boardroom while the patricians were eating petits fours and discussing this and that, attacked them, and took one of their sons who ran away from them and killed him. Spotting Sulla, who was never so valiant as to be a moron, running away, they pursued him down the street with no particularly good intention.

And here's where we once again find ourselves admiring Marius. For where does Sulla find himself? At Marius's front door. And who takes him in? That's right. Marius, who disguises him and ushers him quietly out the back, where Sulla makes his escape and moves on to change Roman history, not necessarily for the better, but there you have it. Later, Sulla denies this whole story, saying something about how he entered Marius's house with sword drawn and got the better of him and blah blah blah. But we don't trust Sulla. He was a toad. It fits with the character of Marius the Roman, the man in love with his own myth and how it fit into the Idea of the corporation, that he would not want his enemy brought low by a bunch of conspirators, even if it would have benefited him personally.

If he was going to kill somebody, it would be fair and square. That was the Roman way, then and now.

It was Sulpicius's day, though, and now in charge of things, at least for a little while, he gave control of the army to his fellow Lefty, the old man of the people, Marius, who must have trembled all over to have been in charge again. He sent his men to Sulla, who was then commanding some thirty-five thousand fully armed veterans, citizen soldiers one and all. And Sulla said, "Nuts," and marched on Rome, becoming the first general to view the army so completely as his private enterprise that it made sense to use it as a weapon in his own interest. Before he set out for corporate headquarters to retake it from Sulpicius, he made sure to kill the tribunes who had been sent by Marius, since at one point or another Marius had done the same to his. Nobody said these guys were nice.

Marius and his son, who coincidentally was named Young Marius, fought for a while against Sulla's forces, but it was no-go. Taking his son-in-law with him, Marius fled Rome, first for one of his country estates downstate and then for the port of Ostia, where he got out of Dodge quick, dropping off home for a brief good-bye and his lunch box and then setting sail for Africa.

His son followed, having escaped with the help of a loyal farm steward in a cart full of beans.

Now begins the most amazing part of the saga, where you marvel at the kind of demented energy that such men possess, the kind that makes it almost impossible for them to view a world without themselves on top of it.

As he fled over the sea, Marius was nervous. They were passing by Terracina, which was ruled by one of his many enemies. But it was, as they say, a dark and stormy night. Everybody was miserable and seasick, and the wind was driving them to the shore. It was a near thing, what with all those rocks and spume, but they made land pretty much at the exact place Marius didn't want to be.

The storm got worse. They were out of food. It was dangerous to stay where they were, and it was dangerous to go inland. They needed to meet people if they were to get food and water. But any people they met could be their last.

Very late, wandering about the hillsides near the beach, they came on a small group of shepherds who recognized them, which is interesting, this being a few years before the invention of newspapers, photography, or television. Be that as it may, they were recognized, such was the fame of the old, wasted man now on his last legs, hungry and cold and wet, running from every armed man, Roman or otherwise, in the civilized and not-so-civilized world.

The shepherds were friendly enough. They told Marius he'd better make himself scarce, since there was a group on horse even then scouring the countryside for him. At this point, his attendants deserted him and went looking for a meal for themselves. Alone, scared out of his mind, Marius ran for a thick forest, where he passed a long, miserable night.

The next morning, famished and desperate, he summoned what strength he had and went looking for his companions and once again summoned the force of his executive personality. He told the group to stick with him. For what reason? Because, he told them, when he was very young he had upset an eagle's nest in which there were seven baby chicklets, or whatever you call young eagles. The augurs decided at that time that this meant little Marius would grow up to become consul of Rome seven times. At that point, standing in the wilderness at the ass end of his rope, Marius had been consul only six times. *Quod erat demonstrandum*—thus it was proven that the crazed, distracted fellow in front of them would one day be consul again, so they should be careful about pissing him off. And guess what? They bought it.

That's management.

Okay, so they're fleeing to no place in particular when they see a bunch of horsemen closing on them from no great distance at top speed. Out to sea, they spy two ships. No place to go. Nothing to do. The group runs with whatever strength they still possess and plunges into the water. One gang of refugees makes for one ship and is taken to safety. But Marius, heavy and exhausted, remains afloat only thanks to the efforts of two servants whose names are lost to history. Little is known about them except, first, that they saved the boss, and second, they probably didn't get any stock options for it.

Marius was then hauled onto the second ship, where he flopped onto the deck like a great, gray fish, heaving and puffing. At that juncture, his pursuers had reached the shore and started yelling at the boat that held its controversial cargo to give him over. Marius wept and pleaded for his life. The captain of the boat first went one way, then another, then at last told the bad guys on the beach to get lost. They rode away, furious. At which point, the captain got a severe case of cold feet, dumped Marius on land somewhere nearby with some bullshit story about waiting for a better wind, encouraged him to go foraging for food and drink, and then, when the old man had his back turned, sailed off, leaving him totally and utterly alone.

Do you know what it's like to be an executive who, after a lifetime of being attended in virtually every activity, is left suddenly alone? I know one ultrasenior officer whose attendants have to zip his fly for him because he has arthritis. Others can't walk half a block without an escort.

So we have Marius on the shore, lying on the sand in silence, in great pain. Famished, enraged, and dejected, he begins to drag his sorry carcass in no particular direction, but figures he'd better move because if he doesn't he'll die.

This seventy-year-old man, used to the most luxurious and pampered existence, now wades through deep bogs, and ditches full of water and mud, and at last finds himself at the hut of a fellow geezer who works in the fens, although it's really tough to figure out what a fen worker might have been required to do. I guess there are jobs everywhere for those who are willing. Marius asks this fellow to help him in exchange for a huge future reward if he is able to effect an escape. His host then takes pity on his visitor, and conveys him to a very secret place where he makes him a bed of reeds and tells him to rest.

Not long after, the horsemen sweep by the hut and beat the crap out of the old fen worker, who coughs up Marius's location. This just wasn't our guy's day. Before long, he hears his death approaching on horseback. At which point he rises up, strips off all his clothing, and dives into a nearby puddle of thick mud. This does no good. He is found, pulled from the mire, and carried naked to the offices of his enemy, who is a pal of Rome— Rome, which is now an enemy of Marius.

The smart thing to do with such guys is to kill them immediately. Amazingly and quite stupidly, they don't kill the crazy, murderous codger, they decide to think about it for a while and, while they are doing so, deposit him in the house of a woman named Fannia. This Fannia had had some occasion to be judged by Marius when he was in his sixth consulship, and had been satisfied with the way she had been treated. Starstruck and merciful, she comforts him, and after hearing him relate some crazy good omen he believes he had received relating to a prancing donkey—never mind—she closes the door to his room and allows him to take his rest, visions of a big comeback dancing in his fat little head. In one version of the tale, the tough old warrior gets to sleep with the woman before drifting off to sleep. I'd like to think that's true.

It gets more incredible. The council of his enemies meets and decides to waste no more time and kill Marius immediately. Only thing is, there doesn't seem to be anybody Roman around who feels up to the job. You can understand why. Finally, they find a Gaul or Cimbrian around who is willing, which is equally unsurprising, per diem consultants being what they are. The assassin goes in with his sword drawn.

The room is dark, and the pallet where Marius lies is shrouded in even more profound murk. Then, from the pitch-blackness, a pair of eyes seems to shoot molten fire and a deep, gigantic voice booms out from the darkness, "Fellow, darest thou kill Caius Marius?" Dropping his sword, the barbarian then turns and runs from the room, yelling about his inability to kill so formidable an executive.

So everybody sits around after this and just plain can't figure out what to do. After a while, the discussion turns to what the man in the dark room has done for Italy through his life. People start talking about pity, and gratitude, and remorse. And before long, they determine that they will simply banish the man rather than kill him, and beg forgiveness from the gods for doing so.

His enemies, transformed by the sheer force of the executive's personality, conveyed him in some honor to a waiting ship, where he made his escape. He headed to Carthage, where he was sent back to sea with some threats from the local magistrate, and then seesawed over a fair portion of the Mediterranean, meeting up with his son at some point, with great rejoicing, and then moving on to continued rootless exile.

Meanwhile, back at Rome, there was infighting, of course, developments that would have a huge impact on our boy and further prove that when it comes to moguls, it pays to kill them when you have the chance.

While Sulla was in Boeotia fighting Mithradates, all the wimpus middle-management consuls started fighting among themselves and some minor player named Octavius, on top for a while, drove Cinna out of Rome for attempted despotism. We don't need to know a lot about Cinna except that he's additional evidence that the corporation at that time, starved for a strong center, was awash in lethal moguls. So Cinna raised an army to get back to headquarters and squash his opposition immediately, and you don't have to be a rocket scientist to know who saw a huge opportunity for the big reversal of fortune he had always known would be forthcoming.

Back came Marius!—setting sail for Italy immediately with blood in his eye and a ton of scores to settle. Coming ashore in Etruria, he was greeted by a huge crowd—the plebes loving a good comeback story. The crafty returning mogul immediately grabbed headlines by freeing the local slaves, exhorted the crowd, and as quick as you could say "You messed with the wrong guy," he had assembled enough fighters to fill forty ships. Plutarch makes one of his funny jokes by observing drily, "Knowing Octavius to be a good man and willing to execute his office with the greatest justice imaginable, and Cinna to be suspected by Sulla, and in actual warfare against the established government, he determined to join himself and his forces with the latter. He, therefore, sent a message to him, to let him know that he was ready to obey him as consul."

Cinna was only too happy to accept the grand old man of the Republic as his proconsul and chief operating officer. Marius now does some really brilliant remarketing of himself. First, he

refuses all the seals and symbols of office, and dresses as a normal soldier, saying his current status does not warrant any more
than that. Next, he neglects to cut his hair and appears shaggy in
public, like a man who has been in exile for a while. All of this is
very impressive in a man of the people, and speaks to the anti-
Senate, antiestablishment populace he and Cinna are attempting
to seduce.

Have we been feeling sorry for the displaced senior officer?
Was our pity moved by his plight? More fools we.

With a new army at his back and fire in his belly, grizzled Marius
made up for lost time. He intercepted ships carrying provisions to
Rome and to his adversaries, plundered them, and swept down on
the port of Ostia, taking it over in unfriendly fashion by killing a
whole bunch of the citizens there, possibly in retribution for
the role the town played in his exile. He then marched his well-
provisioned army to the now cut-off corporate headquarters and
took a nice, juicy position on an advantageous hill.

The existing senior management didn't really stand a chance,
because it played by the honorable rules of the Republic in
which its consul, Octavius, believed. First, he refused to free the
slaves as Marius had done, alienating that large and powerful
portion of the employee base. The army then approached the
young Metellus, son of the man Marius had unjustly betrayed
and then exiled, begging him to take over the fight against
Marius. All stupid and full of honor, Metellus paid homage to the
dignity of the office of consul and angrily told the army to go
back and serve the man who had been elected to that high
office—Octavius! He then left town.

For his part, Octavius consulted some Chaldean augurs, who told him everything was going to work out fine. So he stuck around long enough to be pulled down from his chair in the boardroom and murdered by thugs who had been sent ahead by Marius in advance of his attack on the city. So the old guy won without really ever having to fire a shot, because he was playing the game like he meant it. Against moguls, bureaucracies are at a fatal disadvantage because to them the rules are more important than the outcome.

At any rate, Rome had nothing to do but invite Marius and Cinna in to take over the executive suite. Cinna took the invite in the spirit in which it was given—politely and regally. Marius stood by, brooding. There was no question of what was in his mind.

When they got to the gates of the corporate center, Cinna went in but Marius stayed behind, refusing to enter until the people rescinded the decree by which he was exiled, because, he said, he had too much respect for Roman law to flaunt it in that manner. While the citizens were voting, however, he lost his patience, marched through the gates, and, working with the cadre of slaves he had freed, proceeded to go about the city murdering people, partly by express command but mostly by simply giving his guys a nod of his head. Those who faced him without saluting him were immediately dispatched. Those who did salute him had about a fifty-fifty chance, so that even his friends didn't know where they stood for a while, except for the fact that they knew they were standing ankle deep in blood.

After a while, Cinna got tired of all the butchery and began to think of other things to do, but Marius, our courageous, tenacious, brilliant mogul friend, was just getting started with what was to be the first legitimate terror in the history of organized business. Every day, he sought high and wide for people who might have offended him in the past, for their friends, their loved ones, their gardeners and hairdressers. The roads were full of folks running from the possibility that they might be suspected of something, for to be suspected was to be doomed. As in all such spasms throughout time, in the end it was impossible to trust friend or family member, as the upside for turning in somebody who even momentarily had annoyed you was very great. Brother ratted on brother, manager sold out his junior vice president. Betrayal to Marius was an effective way of getting in with the powers that were and getting rid of the powers that used to be. There was no more Republic. There was a dictatorship of the proletariat, for it had always been the lumpen and working class that had supported this mogul.

The good news for every terrorized Roman, or so they thought, was that Sulla was on his way with a huge army of victorious Italians. He had kicked Mithradates into the sea and taken control of his line operations, extending the reach of the corporation far into Asia Minor.

The old man sat in Rome and waited for the executive action that was descending upon him. His friends, aware that their man would need to be at his best against this most vicious and effective internal foe, elected Marius consul for the seventh time—making the augury that took place at his birth come true. One thing was also certain. There was no prediction that there would be an eighth term. This was it. And Marius knew it.

He was tired and pressed down by his infirmities and anxieties. He grew depressed, like Ted Turner without his lithium. Worst of all, in the shadow of what he knew by experience was to come, he grew afraid. Fear? When had he felt such a thing? Not when he had fled in a little wooden boat against the decree of Sulla and his pals . . . not when he had plunged into the icy mud to escape his tormenters . . . not when he had mounted brave campaigns against the Cimbri and the Teutons . . . but now? He had prevailed one last time against a few pansy togas and their minions, but now he was to face the finest legions in the Roman army. He felt the outcome before the event itself. And his heart sank.

These days things happen in nanoseconds. War is declared and immediately there are unmanned missiles over the lucky nation where the empire is preserving freedom, or creating it where none has ever existed. For Romans, time was a different commodity. The Gauls were coming! When? Next June—six months hence. The Teutons were streaming over the Rhine! We'll take care of them! When? When we get there. Sulla is coming to destroy us and establish a terror of his own! Bad Sulla! Mean Sulla! When would he get here? Six weeks? Two months?

Marius sat up at night, afraid, afraid to sit up and be afraid. And so, like Nixon in his last days wandering around the vacant halls of his corporate center, Marius began to drink, drink vast drafts of wine, obliterating the fear, the yawning hours, giving up. And from his drunken weakness he gave way to pleurisy, and took to walking with a few friends in his garden, reliving past glories, or the events that in his memory had been transformed into glories, and after a while he took to his bed, and after a week, well before Sulla could march into town and give his head a separation package from his body, Marius died.

There are those who say that in those last few days he descended into a form of madness, raging about his offices in a wild frenzy, imagining it was he who had just conquered Mithradates and throwing his body around in a sad mimicry of the postures of battle that had served him so well in the past, filling the rooms with his ferocious battle cries. And most characteristically, although he had been consul seven times and conquered the known world, he complained bitterly of all he had left unaccomplished, all that he had not been given the good fortune and power to do, all that remained unfinished.

In the end, under the egocentric bluster, the mogul always sees himself as a victim, as one worthy of empathy and tender affection. This is part paranoia—they're all after me!—and part self-pity—nobody understands what's it's like to be me!—but in the end, *at* the end, it's the cry of the tiny child inside of every great executive, the one who was never fed quite enough, never honored quite enough, never given the kind of love he or she needed to be a normal person.

In a sane society, such people are dealt with rationally, as sick individuals whose egos need amelioration, either upward or downward in size. In a crazy culture, these pathological titans are promoted, invested with power and respect. Eventually, they destroy themselves, both individually and as a group, giving way to new forms of executive. But the entrepreneurial mogul, the one who defines himself as the state and the state as himself, has amazing power over the lives and imaginations of the corporate culture that gives him birth.

So, seventeen days into his seventh consulship, Marius died, to everybody's great satisfaction. He was succeeded by his son, Young Marius, who to everyone's surprise continued the terror. He in turn was defeated by Sulla, who was even worse. You can't help wondering over and over again, as our corporate tale unfolds, just what there was in the Roman character that made murder as a business tool so acceptable to so many generations of senior management. Perhaps they had their equivalent of *Business Week* on hand, congratulating each CEO on his no-nonsense approach to head-count cuts.

# 7

# The End of the Day

In about the year 63 B.C., not too long after all this took place, Gaius Sallustius Crispus—the soldier, politician, world-class writer-historian and lusty bon vivant we now know as Sallust—wrote about life at Rome, Inc. during the time when crazy republican moguls were running around and the bureaucracy, which had functioned well for hundreds of years, was now insufficient to contain them.

The subject is the conspiracy of Catiline, a relatively minor executive vice president of something or other, against the entire senior management structure to which he was supposed to report. In the following passage, we get a pretty clear picture of what kind of situation Julius Caesar found when he looked at the way everybody in power was zooming everybody else. No wonder he decided to do something about it.

Marius was dead. His hated rival, Sulla, was in power. And everyday life in the corporate center wasn't really worth living even if you were among those temporarily holding the brass balls.

At that degraded stage of the game, Sallust tells us that everybody who was anybody was a robber and a plunderer, each with his own special racket. Some went for houses, others for the one asset that never loses value—land, which was always available even though somebody weaker might be living on it. One of the favorite pastimes of the rich and rapacious was to do a total teardown of the acquired structure and a subsequent construction more to the new owner's liking—just as moguls in Beverly Hills do to this very day.

Many of the miscreants and troublemakers were Sulla's former troops, now at liberty, who were almost as grouchy as he was. Back from extreme unpleasantness hither and yon, they assumed they had the right to roam the city they had defended pretty much at will, thumping, bumping, pillaging, and otherwise painting the town red, literally.

Most evocative is the historian's observation that in this particular version of Roman society—speedy, brutal, materialistic—poverty was seen as a disgrace and wealth was equated with virtue. Innocence and idealism were the lowest expression of bad taste. Sound at all familiar?

As they do now, the values of the elders dribbled down into the generation that was on the way up. Sallust complains (sounding a bit like a right-wing radio talk show host):

> . . . [L]uxury, avarice, pride came to prevail among the youth. They grew at once rapacious and prodigal. They undervalued what was their own; they set at nought modesty and continence; they lost all distinction between sacred and profane, and threw off all consideration and self-restraint.

Sounds like a good time to be young. Nevertheless, does this description remind you of any young people you may know and love? Or are required to hire every day for entry-level positions? Look at that junior director-level fellow just out of Wharton who has just taken up the small office down the hall. How many Jägermeisters did he suck down last night? How many girls is he fucking?

No episode of *Sex and the City* offers a steamier scenario of spicy urban debauchery than do tales of the late Republic. Irregular gratification! Debauchery! Disgusting luxury! Shocking! And why weren't we invited?

Men and women slamming together night and day, sleeping when they felt like it—even in broad daylight; eating when they weren't hungry, just for the sensuous pleasure of it; drinking for no other purpose than to lose their modesty and whatever scant clothing they might be required to wear in the heat of midsummer. Repulsive! Immoral! Why couldn't they stick to the behavior that expressed good old-fashioned Roman values—like killing people in the course of business?

Sallust was indeed ill-tempered about this kind of stuff, particularly since he himself was accused of all kinds of nasty debaucheries by his political enemies. Fortunately his own proclivities didn't stop him from casting a jaundiced eye on others, or we would have been deprived of many a saucy tale.

This may have been a society on the verge of prehistory, but the relationship between license and crime, most often among the very rich, did not go unnoticed. The supreme importance of wealth over stuff like honor and reputation led many young men, when they had run through their fathers' money, to beg, borrow, and steal that which did not rightfully belong to them. A young cadre of violent, highly materialistic young men, stoked on sex and booze, roamed the city. They didn't call them gangstas quite yet.

Enter Catiline, a very bad guy but certainly no worse than many of the people he worked for or who worked for him. He was a man of his age, and alive to the possibilities. At his disposal were these very wastrels of the ruling class, the cream of the corrupt and desperate youth who would do anything for a thrill, a bong, a bit of booty. All of them were in debt. None of them had enough scratch to keep things going without some kind of help from the Man.

Catiline was that man, and he really knew how to recruit. "All assassins or sacrilegious persons from every quarter," Sallust writes, "convicted, or dreading conviction for their misdeeds; all, likewise, for whom their tongue or hand won a livelihood by perjury or bloodshed; all, in short, whom wickedness, poverty, or a guilty conscience goaded were friends to Catiline."

This band of debauched scoundrels represented a solid base of reportees in tune with Cataline's vision of the corporate culture—a huge leg up indeed. But in addition to these, there were quite a few solid citizens prepared to go along simply because they looked at the odds and concluded that Catiline and his guys might win. At least these crazy, vicious bastards had a vision. Things weren't going so hot anyhow. Might as well be on the side of the winners, right?

In a decomposing bureaucracy, it's tough for people to ascertain where their true self-interest lies, and self-interest is the prime mover since there is no other. On the one hand, there is this creep who seems bent on moving into the corner office. Who knows? He may succeed. Then what? On the other hand, there are the other dudes. Which side are you on? Probably the side that pays better right away. That, as we've seen, meant Catiline, who had recently given Marcus Wallibus a Z3 just for the hell of it.

And what was the alternative to the free condo in North Africa and the company chariot Catiline was offering? Despised poverty! We have seen what lack of funds did to your social and political standing in the corporation back then, and it was really no different from any other when you get down to it. Corporations, like the larger social systems within which they operate, have castes. And for the most part, in the absence of hereditary hierarchy, it is wealth that confers aristocracy, power, and the best expense accounts.

In such an atmosphere, it took a very strong middle manager indeed to transcend the prevailing values and remain straight.

So are corporate reorganizations born, through the greed, frustration, and dementia of middle management—and the sheer force of the rogue senior executive with enough moxie to play on it. Catiline doesn't sound like a bad manager, though. He seemed to have the key to his people.

Evil in its free and easy form is a hard strategy to execute, however. It's much easier when you have an edifice of good stuff with which to buttress it. Romans in touch with the positive side of the Force had a whole bunch of inspirational (albeit murderous) ancestors and gods they could draw upon. This made them capable, in the name of all that was Good, of acts of inhumanity that would have appalled the worst sybarite in the employ of Catiline.

The bad guys didn't crave glory, or the greatness of Rome, or fame, or even money, although they assumed that would come later. They just wanted power and the deaths of their enemies. It turns out that this sometimes made them feel bad about themselves. Yes, even in the most sullied corporate center such as this one, the human capacity to feel guilty, to suffer from the weight of conscience, cannot be eradicated. This would seem to be good news, except that in very bad guys like Catiline, this human failing and impediment to the full glory of true corruption leads not to salvation but to an even greater determination to reach their dark strategic goal. Their own evil functions to make them increasingly nutty.

Stewing in his own dark juice, for example, Catiline was accused of corrupting a vestal virgin. This is going way out of your way to be a truly bad mother, and a very big deal indeed—kind of like seducing a nun, only worse, or better, depending on how you look at it. Now we get to the really crazy part:

> . . . [A]t last, smitten with a passion for a certain Aurelia, he murdered his own grown-up son, because she objected to marrying him and having in the house a grown-up stepson.

This is a very great crime, obviously, the kind that seems mythic, apocryphal, like Chronos eating his children. And yet, it happened.

Monstrous crimes such as these end up reaching inside even the most recalcitrant spirit, twisting it inside out, consuming it until nothing is left but ash. And they eventually incapacitate you for public service.

> And this crime seems to me to have been the chief cause of hurrying forward his conspiracy. For his guilty mind, at peace neither with gods nor men, found no comfort either waking or sleeping, so utterly did conscience desolate his tortured spirit. His complexion, in consequence, was pale, his eyes haggard, his walk sometimes quick and sometimes slow, and distraction was plainly evident in every feature and look.

In short, a despicable, nutty, haunted guy, with persuasive powers and a willingness to do just about anything, including murder his own boy when his new squeeze found the younger man's presence a turnoff.

Then as now, great madness brings with it great power. When there is no moderating force to contain the insanity of men—especially young men—virtually anything is possible. The state, which thrives on the cooperation of parties and individuals, begins to slip inexorably into revolution and ruin, and stays there for a while, until the truly insane operators find themselves replaced by the more functional madmen who can get through a day without murdering a family member.

For a while, this extremely potent nutcase and scion of evil succeeded in mounting a quiet, stealthy attack on the ruling structure of the corporation. He had the buy-in of some major Lefties, even, it was rumored, the biggest fish of all, Julius Caesar, well known to be sick of the way business was being conducted. But such support was limited, ginger, one of those things, like, "Hey, I'm with you, man. If you win. Until then, you can leave by the service elevator." Support like that is better than opposition. But it's not worth much.

The problem with a crazy mother like Catiline is that no amount of image work could make him conceivable as a leader of men who valued their reputations, their roots, and their backyard gardens. He simply spelled too much chaos for everybody no matter what party card they carried. He worked well as a conspirator, a thorn in the side, a potential goad to be used by the enemies of order. But nobody wanted to report to him. Catiline as a boss? Get real.

In the end, he came up against Cicero, who was a very adept spinmeister and global positioner. Outed in a series of fabulous speeches that have come down to us in a variety of hardcover and paperback editions that have been forced upon sleepy students for two thousand years, the creepy wannabe was forced to flee to the Jersey Shore, where he was chased down and introduced to the gods of the underworld by the army, which had had just about enough of his ugly face.

The story demonstrates just how badly the state was frizzing out, and how seriously the structure was in need of a strong central executive. But a mid-level pischer like Cataline didn't have the juice to get the big job done. He did make a lot of trouble for a while, attracting the momentary interest and support of much bigger fish of the Left, when they had no other weapon handy to poke the togas. But the system had a bunch of big-time crazy executives that, working within the boundaries of the bureaucratic structure, could easily crush a blunt weapon like Catiline, with his callow band of M.B.A.'s at the ready. The fact that he existed at all was a real bad sign.

Into this moldering infrastructure strode the executives who would make up the last working senior management the Republic would put onto the playing field, men of such incredible stature that we are tempted to say that they just don't make them like that anymore. Except in the case of two of them, they do. These two, who make up two-thirds of the First Triumvirate, were huge, fascinating characters who deserve far better than I'm going to give them here. But in the end? They were both losers:

- Crassus, a gigantic egomaniac, famous for his cleverness, his political acumen, and his amazing gift for making money. He accumulated his huge wealth mostly rebuilding portions of Rome that had burned in one of the many blazes that constantly beset the city. When there weren't enough fires to make his operating nut, he set them himself. An indifferent field officer with good but not exceptional military talent, he became famous from Spain to Asia Minor as the single greediest person in the known world. At several points in his career as a governor of some poor subsidiary of the parent corporation, he pillaged his operation so badly that his bosses were grossed out, which, believe me, was a tough thing to accomplish. In addition to being fabulously wealthy and acquisitive, he was also incredibly cheap. Completely careless of the feelings of others, he was pathologically sensitive himself. He is perhaps most famous as Laurence Oliver, who defeated Kirk Douglas and put the moves on Tony Curtis in the bathhouse.

In the real world, he ended his life on the desert plains of Mesopotamia, where he led a huge Roman army to their deaths because he felt that Pompey and Caesar were getting too much press. When he died, the Parthians cut off his head and poured gold down his mouth to signify their contempt for his greed and his general status as an asshole.

- Pompey the Great: A genius as a youth who simply could not be defeated on a battlefield on land or at sea, a genuine rock star in his day, Pompey was unfortunately not as adept in the corporate suite as he was out there where real work got done. Megafamous when very young, like Jobs in his garage or Spielberg just out of Cal State, the darling scion of the great monster Sulla, Pompey was never able to truly secure a handle on the imagination of his corporate culture after he made his first couple of albums, and afterward was always struggling against men more socially adroit and talented than he. In the end, as a man of the entrenched republican Right, he became a tool of the Senate, which, as we have seen, was perhaps not the smartest strategic move in a culture where that body represented all that was corrupt, flatulent, and doomed. He wasn't a bad guy, though. Just not sustainable. He lost his shorts to the greatest Roman of them all, the mighty Julius, in maybe the most important executive struggle in the history of the corporation. He then fled to Egypt, where he was murdered by a minor toady. His is the story of all the guys in the world who came up just one hand short.

And then there was Caesar.

# 8

# Julius Caesar and the Reinvention of the Corporation

Julius Caesar had the bad fortune—or the good, depending on how you look at it—to see that a reigning corporate culture could no longer sustain the life of the multinational enterprise it was supposed to rule. It had neither rationality, justice, or effectiveness to speak for it, and yet there were still many in the ruling class of the time who could not accept the end of their hegemony. In Caesar, they saw simply the return of monarchy, the end of the putative representative government that represented, in fact, no one but them. And so, on the fifteenth of March, in a year not long before the birth of the simple carpenter whose worldview would one day rule the empire, a group of these middle managers stabbed him to death with daggers. In the end, there were more than twenty gashes on the body, only one of which, directly to the heart, proved fatal. The rest were symbolic.

Like many a corporate coup, those in charge had very little idea of what might follow. They just knew what they didn't want.

The roots of Caesar's assassination lay not only in the

entrenched interests of the class he sought to supplant, but also in the character of the great man himself, for at the end of his days his ego simply took over the rest of his character until, like a goiter, it was all one saw of him.

They always hated him, though, the boys in the executive suite. From the start, he was one of those guys who don't understand who gives the orders, who just do what they want when they think the time has come to do it. This was true of Caesar's career from the beginning, this penchant for strategic thought and subsequent bold action. He made friends when he needed them. He believed in himself. And many a time, he figured, What the fuck—and moved. That's the kind of attitude that gets you killed if you're not careful. Until then, you're likely to do quite well.

Gaius Julius Caesar was born of a noble family in about the year 100 B.C. He had a distinguished career as a young man, first as a priest, which was analogous to one who, as a youth, serves in the Corporate Communications Department of the company, the portion given over to the fabrication of the morale of the enterprise, and then as a promising operative both in the field and at home. From the start, he was a pain in the butt to the ruling class, fashioning himself after the immensely obnoxious Marius, who had had the temerity to suggest that the non-patrician classes might, in the end, be just as qualified to screw things up as their betters.

Around the age of thirty, he decided to get serious. He bribed his way into some positions of power, used the system to get ahead, secured himself good posts from which he could make his mark. For a couple decades or so, he paid his dues in the field, and conquered as none other, not only taking stuff over but also running it very well.

In the year 59 B.C., when our man was about forty, he had maneuvered his way into the post of consul, the highest executive in the land. This may sound impressive, and certainly it is, but keep in mind that the consul served at the pleasure of the sleek, calculating senatorial brass for a year at time.

So, in charge of the best gig in the land, this first of all Caesars immediately used his office to do some interesting things, to communicate a message to his power base—the people. This was a politician of the masses, not the entitled, and a very savvy guy who knew how to play to his audience.

First, he passed a bunch of very popular laws to suck up to his power base, the working rich, the army, and the masses. One measure gave public land to the old warhorses who had worked for Pompey, who had not been adequately taken care of by their old boss, thereby honoring the fighting men of Rome and co-opting a bit of his rival's legacy (and insulting him). He also granted property to the poor citizens of Campania, who presumably appreciated it.

Both moves were opposed by the Senate but supported by Pompey, who possibly didn't understand the weird position he was in, or perhaps lived in the vain hope that if the measure passed he could possibly snarf up a tiny portion of the respect that would flow to its author. Also on hand was Crassus, another man of the people, ostensibly.

Caesar and greedy, needy old Crassus seem to do a lot of business together at the beginning of the younger man's career and the end of the older one's. The fact is, as crazy as Crassus was, Caesar scared him, as he scared a lot of the men in charge. When he was young, for instance, Caesar put Crassus up as the face man for a power move he wanted to make in the Senate. His plan was to go in, hack a bunch of senators to death, and then install Crassus as the top guy with Caesar in charge of corporate security. On the appointed morning, Crassus failed to show up and queered the whole deal.

In an attempt to contain these moguls, the Senate sent the vainglorious Pompey to the east, where he dreamed of being another Alexander, and they gave Caesar an unheard-of five-year sinecure as the proconsul of Cisalpine Gaul and Illyricum, which gave him a lot of very good turf to plunder, if he chose to behave like your average field executive of the corporation at that point. He also got Transalpine Gaul, which promised to be a real pain in the gluteus maximus in the near term, because future French people lived there.

Before taking off for the boonies, Caesar made sure that his enemies in the executive suite were either given attractive postings or dispatched to the next world for a variety of excellent reasons. And then, like superior senior officers then and now, he repaired to a line operation to make the corporation a lot of money and garner continued recognition in the common mind as a genuine operator and not just a fat suit in a big office.

He did well in Gaul and then he did well at home, forming allegiances with friends who were later his enemies and doing what was necessary to become the prime mover in an organization that had a lot of very heavy players. Every time he really got close to the center of power, however, the establishment pulled whatever strings were necessary to keep him in a box. After a time, he couldn't take it any longer. It became increasingly clear that the alternative to success, in his case, was death. He chose success.

Around 50 B.C., sick of the mediocrities in Rome using a variety of horseshit regulations to keep him from the true power he deserved, he drove a small number of highly motivated, loyal, and superbly capable troops into corporate headquarters and took over. When he got control of things, he didn't turn into a cretinous, murderous moron as so many had before him. In fact, he was probably the most active and creative chief executive the company had generated up until that point, and the best in its history if you don't count his handpicked successor, Augustus. That's right, unlike virtually every executive in history, both mine and yours, he was successful in creating a succession plan as well.

The character traits that made Caesar the ultimate business machine were the same that confer the highest levels of achievement in the corporate jungle today:

*Ambition:* When he was a young man on assignment in Spain, Caesar came upon a statue of Alexander, who died at roughly the same age that he was then. Upon regarding this image, Caesar wept, not because he had no more worlds to conquer, but because he hadn't yet conquered any. At that point he quit his job and went back to Rome to establish a more central place for himself at corporate headquarters.

*Lack of sentimentality:* Like many a great Roman, he was willing to use marriage as a tool to power. While still in his training toga, he renounced the professionally disadvantageous plans that had been set up for him and married the daughter of the eminent Cinna, who was consul four times, this for reasons that were obvious, at least to certain reigning powers who resented his ambition. In this latter group was Sulla, a notoriously bad enemy whose favorite form of punishment for those who displeased him was some form of semiofficial hacking to death. Consequently, the young man fled the environs and was forced to hide out in a variety of locations until the situation cooled off, a tactic known to later Italians as "going to the mattresses." In the end, after repeated entreaties from those on the populist side for one of their own party, Sulla relented, with the words: "Have your way and take him; only bear in mind that the man you are so eager to save will one day deal the death blow to the cause of the aristoc-racy . . . for in this Caesar there is more than one Marius." Nobody ever had cause to say that Sulla was stupid.

*Preternatural boldness:* Great executives are not troubled by self-doubt. Until the very end of his life, when he heard the sandman coming, Caesar needed very little sleep, but the sleep he slept was calm and untroubled. Good digestion. Good con-science. Unshakable belief in the myth of Self. That's all it takes. Sadly, few of us are granted even one of these essential assets. Caesar had sackfuls of all three.

And like all great entrepreneurs, the man was absolutely peer-less in determining the exact right time and place for action and, when that was settled, doing what was necessary. The annals are filled with tales of his troops taking on forces five or six times their size and emerging victorious, of Caesar standing in a field of fleeing men and seizing all who came within his grasp and, quite literally, turning them around to fight and emerge victorious, of Caesar plunging into the fray at the head of his army, heedless of his own personal safety, of driving his own horses away so that his men had no choice but to fight and emerge victorious. We have a phrase that exists to this day describing a person who commits himself irrevocably to a bold course of action. It's called "crossing the Rubicon." Caesar did it in the year 49, when, finally sick of the senatorial machinations against him, he determined to take one solitary legion forward to conquer Rome. One legion—against all of Rome! It was a bunch of sissies against the force of destiny.

*Strategic and crafty*: This wasn't a screaming gonzo maniac like Steve Ballmer, though. Once he had set upon his course of action, he did not just hurl himself into the breach. Instead, he set about misdirecting his adversaries and making sure any attack was conducted under such terms as victory was all but unquestioned. In this, he followed the wisdom of Sun Tzu, who in his annoyingly vague ramblings did make some salient points. Perhaps the most trenchant of these involves the idea of not fighting unless you are sure you will win. This is often difficult in the real world. But Caesar did his best to live up to that dictum. Consequently, in his entire amazing career as a corporate acquisitor, he had but three reverses—one in Britain, one in his fight against Pompey, and one someplace else that we don't really care about. None of them added up to much.

That's because he didn't allow his will to drive him to destruction—until the very end, when the executive disease overcame him and he gave his adversaries the intellectual, emotional, and ethical infrastructure to cut him down. This kind of thing is virtually unprecedented in corporate life, by the way—assassination of a chief executive by the established ruling class. Certainly there have been hits before, but they were generally performed by one kind of outlaw or another, not by a bunch of guys in the equivalent of $2,500 suits.

Until he ran terminally aground, however, Caesar never pushed a bad thing to the point of doom, unlike the many Carlies, Kens, and Marthas of our day. He had too much good stuff going on, and he knew it. So he was careful, while never losing his nerve. In Britain, after the destruction of his fleet in a storm on the eastern shore, he ventured only as far as he could without overextending himself. When the outcome of that takeover seemed in doubt, he figured, Hey, no harm no foul, and he returned to France, which he had set up as an ongoing revenue stream, allowing him to accumulate an amazing amount of personal wealth. This he employed to pay off his existing friends and buy new ones. We should all be so lucky to have such a boss.

He was also *a master at stealth and misdirection.* Before crossing the Rubicon, he first sent a few junior executives on ahead of his main force, clearly giving the impression that something was up, but elsewhere. Then he made a great show of touring the site of a gladiatorial school he was thinking of building and sharing a large, public feast with a multitude of retainers, consultants and graphic designers then working on his next best-seller. Anyone looking on as a spy for his adversaries, and we must assume there were plenty, would have been forced to report that nothing was amiss. Actually, he was planning the greatest internal coup in the history of the corporation.

After the sun had set, skulky Caesar snuck out of his headquarters with a small number of trusted lieutenants in a ramshackle cart led by some mules he had secured from a humble bakeshop nearby. During the night, he actually got lost and wandered around in the underbrush for a while, until, at dawn, he was led back to the main road, on foot, by a guide he had happened to meet. At last, on reaching the Rubicon River, which was the outmost boundary of his legal province—where the Senate and its running dog, Pompey, sought to contain him—he still urged caution on his men and pointed out the possibility, even at that late date, of turning around and going back. Anyone who has worked in the corporate headquarters of a large enterprise about to embark on a dangerous takeover of a larger, more formidable organization will admire the lengths to which this great leader went to avoid leaks and catch the enemy with their pants down (even though there were no pants at that point in time). He then crossed the Rubicon and took over the whole game.

*Quotable and pithy:* Great leaders come up with terrific epigrams—not all, of course, but some are real wizards at it. Upon plunging into the battle for control of the company, for example, he told his troops: "The die is cast." That's right, he made that up. In describing how easily he won the battle against Pharnaces, the son of Mithradates, he observed several times, quite openly, that he envied Pompey, who had achieved such a great portion of his fame fighting such feeble opponents, and, when asked to describe the events of that conflict, said simply, "I came. I saw. I conquered." It's hard to imagine an editor finding anything to cut out of that one.

This is not even mentioning his copious writings, which he accomplished while on horseback, hacking away at Gauls, Brits, Germans, and North Africans, or whoever came in his way. The man needed no spin doctors. Imagine if the most admired executive in our culture could write inspiring, detailed descriptions of his activities that could capture the public imagination. These were campaigns that every Roman knew determined the fate of their common civilization. There was nothing more important than what Caesar was writing about. And he produced stuff as regularly as Stephen King did before he was adopted by *The New Yorker* and subsequently hit by an SUV. He did it as a representative of the people, whose interests he passionately represented against the privilege of the senatorial class. That's why, after he was stabbed to death by just about half the Senate, everybody without a country home and a yacht went completely nuts.

Caesar also possessed, in prodigious quantity, *the ability to produce loyalty and achievement in others.* As today, the key to the command of true obedience and loyalty lies in how well the leader can balance the twin tactics of toughness and love. Caesar was brilliant at this. First of all, he called his people "comrades," not soldiers, reminding them that they were all one in the sight of Jove. When they were not in battle, or not in the presence of members of another corporate entity, he pretty much allowed them to do what they liked. At the same time, he had a habit of putting them to work when they least expected it—like on holidays or weekends, reminiscent of Charles Revson's old adage that those who don't come in on Saturday might as well forget about coming in on Sunday as well. He made them march in the rain. He worked their butts off.

Perhaps most important was his absolute lack of fear of his own employees. He slept in a tent close by them. He fought side by side with them. And when they got restive, he waded into the middle of the mob and took them by the scruff of the neck. When at one point a gaggle of sensible veterans were milling about, frightened of the number of adversaries they were about to face in battle, he gave them a little speech. No, he didn't soothe them. Instead, he bluntly overestimated the number of soldiers and elephants they were about to face, closing with the observation that since they now all knew what they were up against they might as well shut up about it or he'd put them all on a boat and set them out to sea. When you think how many executives delegate that kind of thing to creepy subordinates like you and me, you begin to appreciate what a pair of brass ones this guy possessed.

He was also very smart about what exactly makes people love a leader. You and I, perhaps, have good plastic or a lovely company Lexus to remind us why we have a soft spot for our senior executive officer. Caesar gave his war-hardened vets weapons of inlaid gold, tools so gorgeous that they would fight to the death simply not to lose them. Throughout his career, he also gave more parties, dinners, houses, horses, and just plain cash money than any senior manager in the history of corporate rule. One time he was so dissatisfied with a victory dinner he gave for the people of Rome that he immediately gave another, with much heavier hors d'oeuvres. When he died, the terms of his will gave every citizen of Rome such terrific stuff that they immediately were so overcome by a combination of greed and grief that they burned down half the town.

And unlike other nutty Romans before or since, he was *not too vicious, and even merciful at times.* Caesar was by no means an inheritor of the Robespierre- or Dunlap-style terrorism of his predecessors—Marius, Young Marius, Teeny Marius, Sulla, and the like. At the Battle of Pharsalus, where he once and for all defeated the forces of hapless Pompey, he shouted to his troops, "Spare your fellow citizens!" By now, we should be relatively amazed at such a statement. The guy actually had a sense of what Rome could be at that stage of his life, and was motivated not only by a lust for power, but also by a desire to make the organization conform to that ideal. This alone made him unique and precious to the corporation, and dangerous to those who viewed power solely as a means to perpetuate the dominance of their social class.

Still, it was a pretty savage culture, so he didn't have to be Gandhi to win points in this regard. A case in point: When still a youth, he was kidnapped by pirates. While their prisoner, he developed a rather chummy relationship with his captors, who grew to like this charming young fellow, who probably still had most of his hair. They spent their days awaiting his ransom talking, kidding around, playing quoits, whatever, while Caesar fantasized out loud what he would do to them when he was free. So sure enough, Caesar is freed for what turns out to be a relatively pathetic fistful of talents, and the first thing he does is raise a little fleet, chase the miscreants who inconvenienced him down in pretty short order, and, that's right, crucify them. The historians note, however, as proof of his generally genial and merciful bent, that he had their throats cut before he hung them up.

He was also *One Studly Dude:* Business history is full of BSDs,* and Caesar was clearly one of them, with a record of conquest in this regard that mirrored his other activities nicely.

The relationship between sexual prowess—or at least appetite—and business success is well documented and needs no further elaboration in this august venue. Caesar had no moss growing on him, either. What spices up his particular tale is the rumor, bandied about extensively during his lifetime, that he lost his virginity on the receiving end of the staunch affections of one King Nicomedes of Bithynia, a kingdom on the north coast of what is now Turkey, where the young Caesar received some early education in more ways than one. One commentator at the time jibed that Caesar was "the queen's rival, the partner of the royal couch." Another wag had the temerity to refer to him in public as "the queen." And one time, when Caesar was addressing the Senate on an issue of importance to Bithynia, Cicero rose to his feet and exclaimed, "No more of that—for it's very well known what he gave you and you gave him!" At which point we may be permitted to imagine a lusty and protracted hoot from the gallery and a fest of subsequent backslapping at the local bars near the capitol afterward.

---

*big swinging dictators

In fact, rumors continued to swirl throughout his lifetime about his ostensible bisexuality, going so far as to reach the Senate floor, where the elder Curio referred to him as "every man's woman and every woman's man." Interestingly, this didn't seem to hurt his popularity any, either with the public or with the many women over whom he reportedly marched. As befits an executive whose primary job was the acquisition of people and things that belonged to others, he focused on a host of women married to other men.

Not that he ignored affairs of state. His seductions in this arena include the wife of his Mauretanian friend Bogudes, and, of course, Cleopatra, with whom he reportedly spent quite a few all-nighters and, quite possibly, fathered a son, according to as good a source as Marc Antony, who was quoted as saying that Caesar had, in his presence, acknowledged the boy, who actually looked like him.

This would all seem enough for a normal man, but Caesar wasn't any of that. So at the height of his power Caesar went to work behind the scenes engineering a bill in the lower house—asking that it be proposed to the conclave while he was out of town—making it lawful for the boss to marry as many women as he wanted to in order to beget the future leaders of Rome, placing him with Brigham Young and the Sultan of Dubai as a creative thinker on this interesting subject.

He was also *vainglorious:* Oops. Enter the tragic flaw. You remember those. They're the character traits they teach you about in school, the ones that inevitably bring the hero to his sad conclusion. And so it was with our Caesar.

He began with the usual petty bullshit stuff, of course, none of it too damaging. It's amazing to see that then, as now, a mogul's hair was one of his primary concerns. In fact, Suetonius confirms that Caesar, among his many achievements, was the inventor of the comb-over, pushing his "scanty locks" forward to conceal the dome beneath. More hilariously, the scribe points out, "Of all the honors voted him by the senate and people there was none which he received or made use of more gladly than the privilege of wearing a laurel wreath at all times." Caesar was also a bit of a dandy in his dress, adding a fringe to the sleeves of his tunic, which presumably made big news in very early editions of *Vanity Fair*.

Later on, he provided a lesson to all great men and women who surpass their peers and earn the right to believe themselves entitled to an irrational level of exalted treatment. This delusion may be unavoidable in those who move the world. Evidence speaks to that lamentable conclusion. It is always sad to see the greatly gifted, the geniuses, the truly exceptional turn into honking jerks parading around like pheasants exulting in their plumage. And yet, in the end, this was what became of Caesar. His grandiosity stripped the Republic of the illusion of its importance, and that the puffed-up linens of the Senate could not abide.

Before we get there, though, there is a tale of accomplishment that could well be studied by every executive who seeks to be a constructive force, to use power in such a way as to transform his or her little corner of the world for the better. Here are just a few of the things Caesar did in the time that was allotted him—a scant five years at the helm:

- Hired experts to create the 365-day calendar, featuring a month named especially after him

- Filled vacancies in the Senate, stacking the upper house with his guys, much the way Franklin Roosevelt tried to jam the Supreme Court with partisans, and filled a variety of other posts throughout the infrastructure

- Brought back a bunch of executives who had been persecuted by the patricians for fiduciary irregularities, mostly bribery. Since payoffs were about as common in the Roman corporation at that time as they are now in the Far East and the Mob, prosecution of such offenses was highly selective, and usually focused on guys the suits didn't like. In communicating a clean slate, few actions could have been more meaningful to probusiness types

- Took control of the electoral process just as surely as the Bushes took Florida in hand, giving the people the right to elect about half of their representatives, as long as they made up their slate from a list of guys he liked

- Cut down the number of people on welfare—they received free grain from the state—from 320,000 to 150,000, and better regulated who got put on that list

- Decreed that no citizen between the ages of twenty and forty should be out of Italy for more than three years at a time unless it was on military service, keeping the corporate center well stocked with the hale and hearty who might otherwise have gone exploring in the vast world Rome had conquered

- Passed a law mandating that all in the business of grazing must make sure that among their herdsmen were at least one-third of free birth, ensuring that enterprise did not become solely dependent on slaves, a move somewhat akin to Citibank deciding that some of its telephone representatives must in the future come from somewhere other than Bombay

- Made doctors and teachers citizens, improving the status of Rome as a good place to pursue those professions
- Regulated the paying back of debts, not canceling them altogether, but eliminating the usurous hikes that had resulted from the innumerable civil wars in recent years
- Stiffened penalties for crimes, particularly murders committed by the rich; and enforced existing laws on extravagance that limited the kinds of foods that might be sold and served at Roman tables. This fit in nicely with one of Caesar's other traits—a general lack of interest in food and wine
- Imposed duties on foreign products, strengthening local operations
- Kept the citizenry busy with a bewildering array of public works and projects, including the biggest temple to Mars ever, the filling in of a gigantic pool he had himself created for a mock sea battle he had mounted for the public entertainment; the construction of an enormous theater; the regulation of the proliferation of statuary—some of it quite bad—and their location throughout the corporate center; the opening of more and better libraries with the very best Greek and Latin books; the draining of assorted marshes; the construction of a highway across the Apennine Mountains from the Adriatic to the Tiber; the building of a canal through the Italian isthmus; and

many, many more, the number of which were limited only by
his prodigious imagination

Many of these endeavors were put on a back burner when he
was, which seems a shame. And yet, better men than Casca and
Cassius believed it was right to kill him. Not one or two, but
some thirty senators took part in the drill, including the noble
fellow who amounted to his stepson, the high-minded Marcus
Brutus, descendant (supposedly) of the man who had freed the
corporation of its Etruscan kings. A lot more of these dignified
patricians knew about the plot to murder the leading man of
their day, and said nothing. Why?

Because in the murder of Caesar we have the perfect interface
between self-interest and morality, the killer combination of factors that throughout history, from the Crusades to today's com-
puterized versions, has fueled more depredations than all others
combined.

And our boy? Like many a chief executive of more recent vin-
tage, sitting with the weight of the world on his shoulders and,
perhaps, an intern on his knee, Caesar gave his foes exactly what
they wanted.

He accepted all honors that were heaped on him, including
the title of Dictator for Life, a position enjoyed in our day only by
guys who own, not simply run, their corporations.

He allowed the forename Imperator to be given him, as well
as the last name of Pater Patriae—the Father of His Country.
This was very obnoxious to guys who thought *their* fathers were
the fathers of their country.

He was careless in his speech, stating egregious (if true) opinions—like the state was an empty shell, more form over substance; that he was the supreme ruler whose word should be counted as law, that favorites of the past, such as Sulla, were morons, that kind of thing.

When elected officials died in office—even the consul of the corporation—he took it upon himself simply to name a temporary successor, not paying the hereditary dudes the respect they thought they deserved by asking for their opinion. The irony of protecting a republic through its non-elected representatives did not seem particularly piquant to the grouchy elite. He was also fond of:

- The commissioning of statues of himself for holy locations
- Lounging on a raised couch in a special section of the theater
- The wearing of offensively royal purple at all times when a nice magenta would have sufficed
- Sitting in state on a specially constructed golden throne while conducting business in the Senate, whose members continued to maintain a touchy attitude about such gross displays of monarchical splendor
- Constructing temples to himself and placing them beside those reserved for the gods . . .

. . . and plunging other assorted big fat thumbs into the eye of the ruling political and religious pooh-bahs, acts that certainly must have pleased and amused him while being of virtually no utility to the people he had always championed.

In short, he was losing his grip. This happens to senior officers. It's a phenomenon that comes with continued success, age,
and the tendency to surround the chief executive with people
who agree with him as a way to make their living. The number
and range of imperial CEOs who have been revealed as foolish,
vain, hedonistic, or just plain cracked is too long to muster, nor
do I have the wish to offend any of them, since it is part of this
form of narcissism to be not only easily offended, but also somewhat vengeful.

Caesar's power was great. He was nutty and getting nuttier,
but that was old news to those used to a long line of maniacs at
the helm. It was the disrespect, the lack of concern over that
very form that held the Republic together, that emboldened the
righteous assassins.

There were several last straws. When being given an honorary
degree (probably his tenth of that week, at his sixth black-tie dinner), he failed to rise in honor of the Senate. It isn't that he was
against the custom of rising per se. In fact, when a tribune
named Pontius Aquila failed to rise for him at such a ceremony
he flipped his laurel wreath and was reportedly upset about it for
several days, saying to associates that he would only take actions
"if Pontius Aquila will allow me."

Then there was the talk of formally naming him King of Rome.
Sure, he had indicated his unwillingness to take that title . . .
but since of late he had accepted every other title with great
pleasure, there were those who doubted his sincerity. There were
even those who believed he was engineering the move.

Rome had had no kings since Junius Brutus thrust them out

hundreds of years ago. The fact that there was no king was a matter of huge pride to the aristocracy that had filled the power gap
and benefited from the rise of the Republic and the eviction of a
strong, dictatorial monarchy. There was a lot they would suffer to
butter the ego of Caesar. But some things they could not live
with, and being the generation of elite who allowed the return of
kings to the corporation was one of them. As a group, they shared
this conviction above all others, and it had the added benefit of
making them feel good about themselves. No kings. Period.

But Caesar's grandiosity and narcissism was expanding expo-
nentially, like one of those parade balloons on Thanksgiving
morning. Pretty soon there would be no stopping it. So they
began meeting, and in order to appear ethical and moral to themselves, they began mapping out the high tone of the enterprise
almost immediately, calling on concepts of liberty and tradition
and all kinds of very noble stuff. In this effort, they were immea-
surably helped by the participation of several big sheets whose
notion of their role in the world was scarcely less elevated than
Caesar's. In particular there was Brutus, whose life Caesar had
saved on at least one dramatic occasion, and whose mother was
a great friend of the great man. Once Brutus was on board, there
was no question in anybody's mind that they were all doing the
right thing.

In the end, there were more than sixty of the one hundred
senators who came together against him. They plotted and they
met in dark alleys and private homes, and at last they came up
with a plan—to surprise Caesar at the entryway to a theater in
the Senate on the Ides of March.

Caesar himself had ample portents about his upcoming bad day. There were entrails and angry birds and all that kind of stuff, but he had never listened to any of that nonsense during his career, ignoring more auguries than any of his peers, many of whom set their sundials by whatever the sheep guts were saying that morning. He wasn't going to turn chicken-livered now.

So he went to the office that day, even though a bunch of people warned him against it, and truth be told, he didn't feel all that well. For a while, he chatted with some guy who wanted to suck up to him at length, and the assembled conspirators got very nervous that their cover was about to be blown, but it wasn't. It was just somebody bending the chairman's ear, as usual. And as soon as he sat down Tillius Cimber, whose name is now known solely for his role in this great act of liberation, approached Caesar and put his hand on his shoulders, and pulled his toga back, and then one of the Cascas stabbed him below the throat, and Caesar cried out, "Why, this is violence!" and then one by one they all took out their daggers and dove in. At a certain point, Caesar pulled his toga over his head with one arm and demurely adjusted the bottom of his drapery with the other, so that his legs would not stick out unbecomingly when he fell.

When he saw Brutus, his protégé and young friend, approach with the knife, he simply said, in Greek, "You too, my child?" and sunk to the floor and died.

It had been the plan of these courageous friends of the Republic to stand tall and announce to Rome what they had done. Instead, in fear of the monumental nature of their act, they fled, hiding their faces in their robes, suddenly full of dread. For the thing they had done appeared not noble at all now, but terrible, and enormous in its implications. They were also quite nervous, now that you come to mention it, about how the great Marc Antony—by anyone's estimation the number two man in the executive structure—would react. Antony was strong, highly opinionated, not shy about killing people who annoyed him, and especially ill-tempered about matters that were done without bringing him into the loop. The inconvenient thing about Antony, in addition to his grandiose perception of himself, was that (1) he loved Caesar, and (2) he had quite a prodigious army that answered to his every whim. So they thought about what they had done, and they considered the new and powerful enemies they had just made in pursuit of liberty and all that, and they ran away.

Contrary to the wishes of Cassius and the other truly strategic senators, who wanted to throw Caesar's body into the sea and burn down his house, wiser and stupider heads prevailed. The dead leader's punctured carcass was conveyed home. At Antony's house, the fallen demagogue's last will and testament was read, and in it was all the generosity of spirit and love of Rome that had made him, on his good days, the best that the corporate culture was likely to produce. To the people he left his gardens near the river for everyone's use and three hundred sesterces to each man. He also named Octavian his heir, his last creative act, one that quite literally established the future of the empire for nearly a millennium to come.

The people, filled with love for the father of their nation, sickened by the gang-bang assassination, hit the streets and immediately went searching for the murderers. To start off with, they

killed the wrong Casca, but they were just beginning. The griev-
ing and the fires went on and on. During these rites, it is said, a
comet shone for seven days in a row. This was believed to be the
soul of Caesar rising to heaven.

That spirit may have aspired to its Maker, but much of even
greater and more sustaining value to the company was left
behind, a legacy that set the corporation up for the next great
chapter in its global development, one that in many ways
dwarfed all that went before.

# 9

# Antony & Augustus

Poor Caesar. Just as he was about to get all that was coming to him, he got what was coming to him. Unlike many a nutty senior officer, however, he had the great good sense to name a management team to succeed him that actually made some sense. Great of wisdom and insight, and at the same time monumental of ego, he knew it would take not one, not two, but three well-qualified individuals to replace his nonfungible self.

He chose well. For grit and might and loyalty to the people, he chose Marc Antony, and probably also because here was a guy who would keep Rome swingin', full of sweat, blood, and other secretions, not some dour stuffed sheet overly concerned with the public morality. Contrariwise, there was Octavian—young, brilliant, strategic, as cool as Antony was hot. He liked the kid. He wanted him in the picture. And then there was Marcus Lepidus, a pal, a guy he trusted, a boring old bureaucrat who could be counted on to keep an eye on the other two while not being too proud to push the necessary paper around that keeps the machine in gear. Every executive team needs one of these, short on dynamism, long on patience, with the ability to stay awake in meetings while all around them are nodding off and checking the ancient equivalent of their BlackBerrys.

This was the triumvirate that rescued Rome from its bogus, decrepit Republic and delivered it into five hundred years of empire. An admirable team which achieved many great things, for sure. And very noble, absolutely.

But sometimes you've just got to put all that grand stuff aside—and just plain love them. Take Marc Antony. A huge dude. Courageous. Staunch. Loved by his men and hated by everybody else. Very good-looking, with a beard noted for its lushness and shape. Victorious in the field. A total sexual animal, to the point where decent Romans were disgusted by him. Believe me, we're not talking about a willing intern or two. Worse than Jack Kennedy, even, and eventually died for it. Naughty Antony!

Entertaining Antony. Most hilarious, I think, are the tales about his drinking and carousing in the line of duty. On one occasion, he appeared at an important early-morning debate in the hallowed marble atrium of the Senate after a night of wine, women, and general festivity, reeled around the room stoned out of his mind, and threw up in his toga, which was held for him for that purpose by a friend who noticed he was about to hurl. It takes some kind of executive to generate in others the desire to hold a toga in that situation. That's management at its best.

This was not an isolated incident, either. Did you ever know an executive who, for example, did a little coke in the bathroom of, say, Spago now and then? Or could pound back sixteen Gray Geese during the course of a night that ended when it was morning, then button his collar, adjust his tie, and go in with a bunch of Visigoths and kick their butts? If you have not, I pity you. Crazy gonzo fruitcakes like Marc Antony make it exciting to be doing the work of a great corporation.

He was also generous, as generous as Elvis, come to think of it. One time, on a whim, he gave some buddy of his a big chunk of cash right out of his own pocket, from the sound of it I'll bet it was like a $5 million bonus in 2006 dollars. His controller, grossed out, actually got the money out of the vault and piled it up to show Antony the size of it when next he reeled by. Spying the pile right on cue, our lascivious, drunken hero paused, looked over his crimped little finance VP, and said, "I had no idea I had authorized so paltry a sum. You'd better double it."

Great guy. Slept on the ground with his men. Never said die, until he did. Always the only one to show up with a hundred boats and fifty thousand troops exactly when you needed him. But a CEO? Never. The true CEO is made of sterner stuff. While Antony, big, full of life, a man of action and juice, was downing a side of beef and calling for somebody else's wife to come back to bed, there was another, quieter senior officer, very young, very serious, having a small crust of bread and a mouthful of slightly sour grapes on the way to a lukewarm bath.

This would be Augustus, the executive formerly known as Octavian. From the start, purely CEO material. Very early on attaches himself to Julius Caesar and supplants Caesar's favorite limo companion at the time, Antony. We can almost hear the older officer going "Grr."

Slight of build, almost too handsome, if you know what I mean. Looks like a big guy, though, according to contemporaries, unless he is directly positioned next to someone taller. This is not surprising. The illusion of size is often a key asset of short superior officers. (In one of my other books, there is an impressive list of short guys who have moved the planet. If you like this book, I'm sure you would find it equally entertaining.)

And Augustus wasn't just short, particularly when standing next to Antony. He was, in fact, a geek, always noodling away at something in a funny hat he liked more than any other, hiring boring speakers to torture his dinner guests with long, speculative conversation, always complaining about his health, which often waylaid him when things were at their hairiest. At times, particularly in the early battles right after Caesar's assassination, his behavior is vaguely reminiscent of the knights in *Monty Python and the Holy Grail,* the ones who, when attacked with any level of ferocity, turn and—with repeated cries of "Run away! Run away!"—run away. He was kind of known for it, and Antony, never slow with a good-natured corporate jibe, did not hesitate on many occasions to call him a sissy.

As usual, Antony was missing the point. Geek bosses have bestridden the earth throughout history, and they rule the planet today, where their numbers include:

- Bill Gates: What would our world be without him?
- Steve Jobs: Is there a more creative and productive mind?

- Andy Grove: A wonderful man who runs one of the truly great corporate enterprises.
- Dreamworks SKG: Every one of them.

My point is, to many, a short leg is just as good a lever as a long one. So while Antony swaggered, slapped backs, and swapped skin with his buddies as he made his sometimes smelly way through the Senate atrium, kicking up a ruckus and making serious people grouchy, Augustus was standing quietly in a luminous corner of a magnificent public space, where the light hit him best, quietly amused, wondering how long he would have to put up with this garrulous, crafty, powerful asshole before he had the juice to arrange his exit package. It took sixteen years.

Being Octavian was okay, although Caesar sometimes got a little fresh in the limo. But being Augustus was better, now that his rabbi was gone. That was a real solid the old man did for him. Who was he to reject the honor of name, as some statesmen—who would soon be dead!—had suggested?

And so Octavian became Caesar Augustus, and later completed the rebranding effort by boiling it down to the nub: Caesar—the first who made the title as important as the family name. The one. The only. There was Augustus, and then there was everything after. When he died, they made him a god. There has never been a better CEO.

At the end of his life, Augustus wrote what he believed to be a "book" of his great achievements. It's a very tiny little thing called *The Deeds of the Divine Augustus,* and was written when he was seventy-seven years of age, which is about one hundred forty-five in the dog years of Roman politics. The truth is, you feel how bored Augustus was when he wrote it, even though it was a labor of love. His way was to act, to forge, to smelt, to lay rail and hew stone, in short, to do, not to trumpet his way onto the best-seller list like a showboating Trump—although he did have the whole text inscribed in golden columns and displayed in the Forum, as any true mogul would.

What a lot of deeds there were, too, starting when other guys were still out getting laid and wassailing. At nineteen, for example, he raised an army and set the state free of the small, entrenched faction that was running it. He did so, he is careful to note, at the instigation of the Senate and the people, and at his own expense. Such a polite god!

He kicked the murderers of his father-uncle out of Rome in a fully legal manner, dotting all the necessary i's and crossing whatever t's he came to, and when those rotten traitors turned like the weasels they were and attacked the benevolent state, he swiftly conquered them in two battles—one in which Cassius was defeated and the other that drove the noble revolutionary, Brutus, to his suicide at the hands of a slave who had been hired for that specific purpose. In Augustus's version, Antony had no hand in these victories, but the truth was he pulled Octavian's ass out of the fire repeatedly, with an unprecedented record of bravery, daring, and plain blind luck. For his part, Augustus was very proud that although he waged war "over the whole wide world," and was always victorious, he was generally kind to the defeated. This is sort of true, except when it wasn't. He was better than most.

He received two ovations, which were a very, very big deal, three triumphs, and was named emperor twenty times. All these title-related rituals meant very specific, important things to the Roman hierarchical culture, much as a promotion from senior VP to executive VP can put the wood in a contemporary executive's pocket for years. Rome kept giving Augustus the same fantastic titles over and over again, simply because it had sort of run out of things to confer on him. Each time, he thanked the Senate, the people, the gods, you name it. He wasn't about to make the same mistake his punctured predecessor had done. Cultures need myths, and central to this corporation was the myth that it was a free republic. So he was always nice to his board.

In thanks for his wonderful deeds, the Senate threw parties for the immortal gods in his honor fifty-five times. That's a lot, but it pales beside the 890 days on which the Senate decreed there would be lesser sacrifices. He was consul thirteen times and tribune, which was not emperor but was not chopped liver either, for nearly forty years running.

Yet while he ran the whole show from Sicily to the Norse country, he never, ever agreed to be dictator or king for life, although that in fact was what he was. He had statues to himself taken down from Hispania to Syria, once again sucking up to the Roman idea of itself. He also shared his offices on many occasions with bureaucrats who I'm sure gave him no trouble whatsoever, any more than a ceremonial Governor for the Day in Sacramento is likely to enact serious local legislation disagreeable to Arnold.

He added a significant number of new blood into the ranks of middle management, and conducted a census on a regular basis of his growing corporate center. Between 29 B.C. and 15 A.D., under his leadership, Rome grew from four million to nearly six million happy pagans.

To keep them in the pink about themselves, he spearheaded an ongoing campaign to reintroduce, promote, and refresh the branding of the entire zeitgeist, bringing back some of the culture's favorite festivals, religious observances, blood sports, and moral standards that may have lapsed in the dirty old days of the old Republic. It was no wonder that throughout the city, prayers were continually offered for his health at all public shrines and temples. Geek that he was, Augustus tells us exactly how many such prayers were offered and at what locations, a fact that should be instructive to those who believe that CEOs can't be great detail people.

There is also a numbingly tedious list of assorted statues, noisy declarations, and pompous consecrations, with attendant public huzzahs whose import is as inscrutable to us now as the 1986 Malcolm Baldridge Award for Quality that sits on my desk in New York City would be to any Roman citizen, and possibly even to you.

Although not as spontaneously generous as Antony, who was forever giving Cadillacs to passing strangers, Caesar paid a mother lode of raw cash to Rome and to every breathing Roman over a period of years, an amount, by the end of his reign, that makes David Geffen look like a complete cheapskate. He paid for grain and gave it out to everybody, paid for the land he needed to give his soldiers when they came back from the latest bout of hacking and slashing, paid about 600 million sesterces for Italian

estates he could simply have seized and 260 million for provin-
cial fields that were his for the taking if he wanted to be a dick
about it.

Four times he helped the senatorial treasury—150 million sesterces, not to mention 170 million to the military treasury, his
own dough, not the state's. Everybody got a taste; nobody who
was loyal did without. In the end, the money he spent on various
public treasuries, discharged soldiers, or gave to the Roman people directly came to 2.4 billion whatevers. I don't think anybody
hates a senior officer who gives out those kinds of incentives, no
matter how big a bonus he takes for himself.

And he did. Augustus lived well, and supported a load of
greedy, needy, nutty relatives in fine style, executing far fewer of
those who were brave enough to get near him than any Caesar
before or since. This equable nature did not extend, sadly, to his
daughter, Julia. Treating her like one of his conquered dominions,
he forced his poor little rich girl to marry so many of his political
cronies—sometimes when she was pregnant with the current husband's child—that she eventually became a total slut who did
nothing but party until the neighbors complained to Management.
Enraged and humiliated, the angry father banished the daughter
he had ruined to an island where he would not have to look at her
or hear about how many men she had sex with the night before.
He never forgave her, either for her bad morals or her bad taste,
it is impossible at this remove to say which.

While he was screwing up his family, as so many great leaders
seem to, he kept himself pathologically busy, building hundreds
of great-looking buildings, including many temples as well as fun

stuff like malls and theme parks. Many he constructed with his own money—without, he observes, putting his name on it. Aqueducts, bridges, roads, entire cities, eighty-two temples, indeed anything in the whole empire that needed rebuilding— theaters, basilicas, temples to Apollo, to Jupiter.

He also sponsored an amazing array of world-class artistic talent, including box-office behemoths like Ovid, who produced material that would not have conformed to broadcast standards, Horace, who is now too boring to read, and the George Lucas of his day, Virgil. Most amazing was the great patron's tolerance for work critical of his majestic self. Virgil, for instance, began his career with a work that was highly critical of Caesar's policy of granting land to returning soldiers, and his great epic was the *Aeneid,* a very long poem indeed that demonstrates a distressing lack of enthusiasm for wars of conquest, even those authorized by a benevolent state. Still, there was nothing Augustus loved more than befriending and supporting show business people and truculent artists. As we have seen, many nights he would put his guests into cardiac arrest by forcing them to listen to lengthy readings from one worthy scribe or another. He believed in a life of the mind as well as of the stomach and the sword.

To make sure nobody had any time to think about anything subversive to the operation, he also provided a lot of gladiatorial stuff that should really turn your stomach unless you're a very seasoned business type indeed. Romans were glorious and all that, but as a bunch of repulsive perverts they were second to none. I'm sure you've seen the movies. All that wasted human life. Huge crowds of yelling citizens watching terrified dwarfs fighting glandular giants in funny costumes, children being murdered by their parents. Doomed men pounding each other's brains in. Lions killing tigers, dogs howling in pain, elephants screaming and crying, and assorted chickens, warthogs, and occasionally women and children being chased around and dispatched. What's up with that? Augustus brags about the number of beasts from Africa that were killed. More than thirty-five hundred! How about that?

And finally, he solidified the holdings and established a peace that lasted for a long time, because it established a company that was *impervious to its senior management*. That's saying a lot.

This was the Rome you wanted to live in. It was free of pirates at sea, didn't have to worry about slave rebellions, which were a big worry for hundreds of years, because he pardoned about eight hundred thousand of the rebellious and, in exchange for their loyalty, gave them land, helped them start new cities where they could become the kind of rich Romans you and I would like to be one day.

Not just Italy—Gaul, Spain, Africa, Sicily, and Sardinia all bent their knee and held out their hand for a boost into the good life. The world he created was safe for Romans from the mouth of the Rhine on the east north to the land of the Cimbri, who had been extremely obnoxious in the past but were now eager to join the list of pleasant subsidiaries and trading partners. South to Ethiopia! East to Arabia! Armenia—where he conquered and then reinstalled the local king, making a friend for life. A little slaughtering here. A fistful of dollars there. Pretty soon it was all Rome, and that was a beautiful thing, and nary a hand was lifted against his neighbor in anger, and the money flowed back and forth, and nobody didn't get the concept of the corporation.

Truly awe-inspiring. I also like another story about Augustus, the wise man, sage, and genius of his age. During his early phase as a work in progress, the young warrior, very much inventing himself at the time, his career teeming like a chocolate-covered stick with enemy ants, many of them his closest friends and part-ners, oversaw a fairly extensive putsch of the Roman ruling class. He wasn't the only one at the helm, of course. His very best friend of the moment, Marc Antony, was right by his side, with an equally long list of proscribed executives that the two hon-chos, along with their elderly butt-boy Lepidus, decided had to be expunged. Nearly a thousand statesmen of various sizes got stabbed, poisoned, or thrown off cliffs before it was over. The truly honored were forced to kill themselves. Precisely how this was done is unclear—threats? cajoling?—but it would clearly be a useful line of research for those on the cutting edge of human resources management to pursue.

In any corporate transformation, a good housecleaning is absolutely called for, no senior manager in charge of one will con-tradict me. The old bosses are dead and gone. You are the new wave, the guys who have the ideas and the resources to imple-ment them. All around you are these hostile, dangerous husks of the former team, talking the talk but in no way walking the walk. Yes, you can live with them as they undermine every trestle you build and plot secretly to bring back some reactionary, rear-guard structure—or you can kill them. There's a name for those who fail to do so. They're called losers.

It's not a pretty part of the job, though, and nobody really gets into it. Much. Which brings us to Augustus, normally quite a cool cucumber, who for an unimportant reason got extremely angry with a former associate one day in the midst of the execution of his restructuring plan. Not content simply to condemn this gentleman to death, the Father of His Country, later deified, reached into the skull of the unlucky former department head and personally plucked a juicy eyeball from its throbbing socket. Ouch. That really hurts.

I've known only a few folks who could rip out a fellow employee's eyeball, and they are all CEOs. You've got to be willing to do things like that if you want to take a bunch of strong individuals in hand, many of them great and vicious egotists themselves, and scare them so badly that they will do whatever you ask them to do, no matter how demented, rather than risk your displeasure or, contrariwise, to earn your praise.

Anthony possessed it too, that ability to control an entire field full of armed men through a potent combination of love and fear, bring them to their knees in tears in an orgy of hysterical loyalty, begging to die for you. With Antony, it was always about the heart, though. His heart is what did him in at the end, the big lug. For Augustus, feelings had nothing to do with it. It was business, not personal.

A face-off was inevitable. And not having the benefits of foretelling the future no matter how closely they studied the chicken guts that sizzled in the fire, or eagles that circled overhead, or the weather, or their dreams, the outcome of this great contest was anything but clear to anybody right up until the very end.

At the start, the day after Big Julie is stabbed by a group of men whose careers he made possible, you'd have to say the corporate table roll was not that hard to read: Antony, big and strong, crazy and drunk and full of lust, with an army of jackbooted behemoths at his beck and call, is clearly the man to watch. But there's this skinny little kid who's got no army to speak of but walks around talking like he's Caesar—and the thing is? He is! He's Caesar! Who said so? Caesar! Chew on that for a while, if you're sitting around working for Antony's side of the company.

Even before the old guy got his severance deal, Antony was worried about the whole Octavian situation. There was something funny about the little fella. Like, how did he worm his way into the big dog's heart so quick, stealing his attentions like a little queen? Okay, he was charming, the little fuck. But why had the old man made this untested boy his heir, given him his name, for the love of Jove. Caesar! What was the value of that brand with the Roman people? It was everything! How could the Boss have done it to him? He, Antony! It seemed like only yesterday that they were coming back from that huge deal in Spain. More than a hundred top Romans came out to meet the executive convoy, and who had stepped out of the Maybach with the chief executive? He, Antony! Right after Caesar. And now here comes this little Octavian shitbag, with all the goodwill of the corporate logo at his back? Fortunately, there wasn't anything he could do with it. He wasn't even twenty, a scrawny little geek, too. A fellow player at headquarters, to be used and controlled as necessary or, if possible, killed. He would wait. Things would work out.

And they did, for a while. Octavian, ever the serious manager, went about his business, fortifying his positions, making friends, not really getting in Antony's way except when they had an internecine skirmish now and then. When the former Pompey's son, Sextus, was making a pain of himself in Sicily, it was Antony who joined with Augustus to put the corporation back in the black, as he had done after the assassination, when his craft, duplicity, and passion had engineered a public renunciation of the act.

It wasn't only Augustus who knew how to wheel and deal, who was willing to lie and position to get what he wanted for Rome and for himself. Antony was a smooth operator too.

Just not smooth enough. He had always been a slave to his appetites, from the time he was a young executive wandering the town with his friend Curio, who always seemed to know where there were a couple of babes and some frosty brew to while away the hours between dinner and breakfast. Now, well . . . Rome was sort of a bore, wasn't it? Who wanted to be back at corporate headquarters, planning other men's battles and going home at night to Fulvia. Why had he married her, anyway?

So Antony went off to fight the enemies of Rome in the east, leaving the other guy to do the crappy managerial stuff back at the office. Let 'em have it! There were bigger jobs to do than push a lot of parchment around behind a desk, right? The friggin' Parthians were still at it—they would simply not be acquired! Stubborn mothers! They had lured Crassus and his entire army to its death in the desert, expertly playing on the old idiot's vanity, surrounding his men and impaling them, one by one, with arrows. And now they were up to the same deal—defending themselves, killing the good guys, running spies, manipulating local assets, driving Rome out of Parthia and back into Armenia in a hail of blood. That bastard King of Armenia wasn't much better, the little weasel, promising support and then going on a fishing trip at the last minute. No, attention needed to be paid to Asia. There are times when being on the road is a lot of fun. This really wasn't going to be one of them.

That was all right, though. Antony was up for the battle. He was a senior officer at the height of his powers, insight, and persuasiveness over other men. He was that rarest of beasts—a boss who was also a good guy. Flawed, sure. A bit too susceptible to the kind of expert sucking up that is practiced at the highest corporate levels. Not always solid in his judgments. But a human being among the suits.

"There was a simplicity in his nature," wrote Plutarch,

and slowness of perception, though when he did perceive his errors he showed keen repentance, and made full acknowledgement to the very men who had been unfairly dealt with, and there was largeness both in his restitution to the wronged and in his punishment of the wrong-doers. Yet he was thought to exceed due bounds more in conferring favors than in inflicting punishments. And his wantonness in mirth and jest carried its own remedy with it. For a man might pay back his jests and insolence, and he delighted in being laughed at no less than in laughing at others . . . Such, then, was the nature of Antony, where now as a crowning evil his love for Cleopatra supervened, roused and drove to frenzy many of the passions that were still hidden and quiescent in him, and dissipated and destroyed whatever good and saving qualities still offered resistance.

The jury is out on whether Cleopatra was the exquisite siren of fiction. Chances are, she wasn't. Reports were that she had a big nose. Her face was more noted for its character and intelligence than for the perfection of its proportions. Recognizing that sex was every bit as important a tool of statecraft as swordcraft, it's still pretty clear that in working to manipulate this large, emotional Roman she herself was acquired by his personality as well. They were united from the start by some powerful common attributes:

- Amazing manipulators: Each had a long history of getting what they wanted through a combination of charm, determination, and sex appeal.
- Lovers of food and wine: They formed a club dedicated to high living, which continued until the very end of their lives, when they disbanded it and formed a new club dedicated to death.
- Sex maniacs—there's no other way to put it: Their behavior in some key situations is far too demented to offer any other explanations, particularly Antony, who spent the better part of his last years going in the direction pointed out by his erect penis.
- Power players: Each had been in charge of their action for most of their adult lives. They knew where the bodies were buried on their turf because they had buried most of them.

- Heedless morons: Neither could be told what to do once they got their game plan into their heads.

It's kind of sad and funny to see how these two gigantic players fell into each other's thrall and in so doing conformed exactly to the shape of Augustus's long-term strategy. Like so many great men and women from that day to this, they were destroyed not by the concerted efforts of their enemies, although those certainly played a part. They were brought down by themselves, their own inability to be anything but themselves. Would Nixon have been laid low if his paranoia hadn't forced him to place a tape in the Oval Office? Would the guardians of the Right have been able to disempower a more recent Antony if they hadn't been given an intern to play with?

The tale of these two gives us an opportunity to watch a pair of consummate experts zooming each other, and after a while, it's really tough to tell who is zooming whom.

It started out fairly routinely. Antony, waiting to get going on yet another Parthian campaign, calls for Cleo to come explain why she was so chummy with Cassius, who had recently fallen on his sword, and not in our current metaphorical sense of the term, either. The messenger sent by Antony, recognizing that she was a stone fox, advised the Egyptian queen on how to deal with his boss. Dress nice, he said. Hold a fancy dinner. Use the same tools you employed to snag Julius Caesar way back when. You're going to get more from this bee with honey than you will with vinegar.

And so she went, in a barge with a gilded poop and sails spread purple, arrayed in silks and all sorts of jewels, with big sweaty slaves fanning her and virtually naked ladies draped as mermaids festooning the deck all over the place. And Antony, the dumb yutz, cogitating this display with all the probity his pecker would allow, thought, Wow. What a babe.

Those on the shore looked on in shock and awe, and the rumor went around that Venus was about to hook up with Bacchus for the good of Asia. Then as now, people really love a good celebrity matchup.

He invited her to supper. No, she said. You come to me. He figured, Hey, why not.

Her barge was arrayed with thousands of lights. She looked very beautiful. There was more food than it was possible to consume, and a great deal of wine. She was clever. She was bold with him, since she had been told that he would respect her more as an imperious queen than as a respectful subject. He had enough of those.

The next day, he invited her over, but felt embarrassed at the simplicity of his setup there. No lights. The eats were fine, but nothing like hers.

They talked. She had a tremendous sense of presence about her, and the quality of a soldier, too, just like him. But ah, that voice. There was something about it . . . sweetness, yes, but a little gravel underneath. And how many languages she spoke! Whoever encountered her, whether they be Ethiopians, Troglodytes, Hebrews, Arabians, Syrians, Medes, or Parthians, she spoke with them in their native tongue. A very smart woman, then. Smarter than he, really. That was a turn-on, too. And experienced. Very. Made him a little jealous, which is always a spicy addition to the sensual mix. Impossible not to listen, then, and dream, and be fascinated, and, in the end, to love her as had just about every Roman executive who had encountered her.

In a strong, male-dominated culture such as . . . well, what isn't? . . . an attractive, bold, intelligent female executive can wield an awesome amount of raw power over the tiny titans who are trying to think about serious things and not be overwhelmed by the scent of her perfume. I have watched budget meetings, mostly in the 1980s, when such women were far more rare in such settings, in which a peek of leg sheathed in silken hose was enough to ratify the expenditure of millions. Guys drool, that's the basic takeaway, and corporate guys drool worse than most. The more statesmanlike they're supposed to be, the worse their mouths do foam when the proper stimulus is supplied.

They had a lot of fun while it lasted. With a wife back in Rome fighting for his interests against the crafty, patient Augustus, Antony basically went out to lunch for a couple of years. When they would have a dinner for a couple or sixteen friends, he and Cleo, the chefs would have to prepare enough for a hundred people, not because the party would eat that much, but because multiple meals had to be made in stages, so that all would be immediately available when called for. They partied. They had a blast. They made love all over the place, and had two children they thought would rule the world.

And most of all, she never left him alone. She played dice with him, and drank with him, draft for draft, and hunted with him, and watched him when he exercised, and when he hit the town late at night to hang out with the downscale homeboys of

Alexandria, she dressed like a guy and went with him. What a woman!

One time, he went fishing, there being not much to do at the office that day, presumably, and naturally Cleo went with him. He wasn't catching much, and this annoyed him, he liked to look like a stud in front of his squeeze, so he instructed a couple of slaves to dive down and put a few fish on the end of his rod. These he reeled in to the oohs and aahs of his love, who knew exactly what was going down. Next day, bringing along a few of her pals, Cleopatra once again set down to watch the ruler of the East give it another shot. Only this time she had arranged for a fish of her own to be applied to his hook. Antony, excited and pleased by his immediate success, reeled in the fish her divers had provided: a salted herring; and there were big laughs for one and all, and lest her man feel in any way slighted by this saucy gambit, Cleopatra said, "Imperator, hand over thy fishing rod to the fishermen of Pharos and Canopus; thy sport is the hunting of cities, realms, and continents." See? Do a little dance. Make a little love. Get down tonight.

You can't say Augustus was a bad guy about Antony. He gave him a real chance to pull himself out. Worried about the influence Egypt was having on his fellow consul, he invited him back to Rome, made sure they were all square about things, and arranged, after the somewhat convenient death of Antony's wife, Fulvia, who neither of them liked much, for the marriage of his partner to his own sister, Octavia. And while Cleopatra was a blinding gem in the diadem of the corporation, there was no moss on Octavia, either. She was extremely beautiful, dedicated to Rome, a devoted mother to all of Antony's children, including those who were not her own, a true and excellent wife. She got very little out of it, although it is possible to see that Antony did like her a lot, and feared her disapproval. As he reeled toward his doom, he always made sure that Octavia was on the other side of the Mediterranean from wherever he was at the time.

There were a great many campaigns and battles and you can bet that Augustus got pretty sick of the way his sister was being treated, once Antony managed to escape from corporate and find his way back to Egypt and his one true love. It was when the big dummy started giving away subdivisions of Rome to his other family, however, that Augustus was forced to move against the guy whose empty office at the other end of the floor yawned wide each and every morning when the CEO came to work. He wasn't doing that well on the operating end of things, either. The guy had become a total waste.

Their forces met at Actium, which is off the Grecian shore, and it was a naval battle, even though Antony commanded ground troops far in excess of those of Augustus. Why? Because Cleopatra wanted him to. Something about how it would look, more grand, more spectacular to enter the battlefield in their huge, splendid ships, which in fact were grossly undermanned because there were so many of them—again for show. So Antony's one hundred thousand land-based soldiers and fifty thousand horsemen sat around twiddling themselves and Caesar's fast, well-staffed, nimble ships met Antony's lumbering display vehicles head-on in the mother of all sea battles.

It was touch and go for a while. And then something pathetic and amazing happened. In the middle of the fight, when it could still have gone either way, Cleopatra got frightened, gave the signal to her ships, and sailed away from the field of action. And Antony, with his men fighting and dying by his side, with the outcome of the engagement still very much in doubt, called for a small, fast boat and went running after her. He bailed.

Antony arrived at Cleopatra's fleeing boat and hauled himself up onto the deck. But he did not go to her. He sat in the rear, on a simple bench, his head in his hands, for many hours, weeping, feeling his disgrace, his inability to do anything to expunge it. He did not kill himself, as he might have, because he still loved her and wanted to live as long as she lived. He did not reenter the fray. It was too late for that. He could not face her, too full was he of shame and anger and confusion. Who had done this? Could it have been he, Antony, the bravest of the brave? No! Who was he, then, if he was not Antony?

So he curled into himself and wept while his forces fought bravely on and, when they became aware that he had fled, battled on still in disbelief, and then died, because they were destined to, having been created and trained more for display than function.

Antony sat on the deck for several days, eating and drinking nothing, an empty shell, until his servants and hers got together and came to him and convinced him that he and Cleopatra were better off together than apart. So they slept together again, and perhaps it seemed all right for a moment or two, although they knew it wasn't.

That was the end of Antony. Even with the greatest army in

the world still under his command, he initiated very little of importance. He had been unmanned. Executive power comes from the belief of the individual in himself. And that is what the poor, sad mother had lost.

He wandered the world for a while, alone, occasionally with a Greek philosopher or two, and you know what that kind of thing can do to you. He had lost everything, including the daily joy of being in love with the splendid woman of his dreams. It was all poison now. He went back to Egypt and found Cleopatra trying to move her ships by land across Egypt and into the Red Sea, to avoid Augustus, when he came. He helped with that for a while, and they hung out together, and talked about death, how they would die, and when.

Caesar wasn't long in coming. Always the superb executive, he saw his chance to complete this last phase in his corporate reorganization and took it.

One day as they waited for his arrival and their fate, a rumor came to Antony that Cleopatra had taken poison, and was dead. Dead! What a good idea, he thought. Once more filled with shame and grief at being the second in line for a dramatic action, Antony took his sword and ran himself through, rather than either fight, be taken captive, or live in a world without his one true love.

Except she wasn't dead. And by the time he learned this, it was too late to put his guts back. Because unlike the job he had done on hundreds, perhaps thousands of others, Antony did a lousy job on his own suicide. That is, he didn't die right away. With his entrails spilling out all over his hands, his clothing soaked with blood, he had himself carried like a baby to the secret tomb in which Cleopatra had hidden herself and fell into her arms.

She wrapped herself around him, sobbing, deranged with grief, and tore at her breasts with such ferocity that in the days preceding her suicide there were great fears that she might in fact die of those wounds.

She anointed his body and cremated it with great care. And when Caesar arrived, and promised her respect and kind treatment were she to return politely with him to Rome, she was demure and cordial, asking only that she be allowed to observe appropriate funeral rites for her beloved. But she was lying. She had no intention of going to Rome as a captive. She had, as was her practice, done a thorough investigation on the easiest way to die, and determined that the bite of the asp was relatively painless, and that the ensuing death was swift and involved little more than a gradual slide into lethe. And one day she had a basket of figs brought to her. The basket was searched carefully, presumably, as security people check our carry-on bags today for things that might hurt people, hopefully to better effect, for there was an asp in a space beneath the figs and that was the end of Cleopatra.

Augustus wept when he heard the news of Cleopatra's death, and he decreed that she and Antony should be buried together in Alexandria, with full honors, which was really saying something in those days when the manner of interment determined one's status in the afterlife in both Roman and Egyptian corporate culture.

And then Augustus went on to do all those deeds we know

about, plucking out a minimum of eyeballs after he grew into his true self and provided the living proof that excellence is possible in a leader who cultivates not his human capabilities but his executive ones.

He had his burdens to bear. His wife Livia, for instance, was a serial killer who focused on inconvenient family members who stood in the way of her son Tiberius's accession to the throne, for a throne in truth it now was.

What a leader, this Augustus. Maybe the best ever, if one believes that leadership is essentially a creative enterprise that builds value for all citizens over the long term, not simply a short-term means of providing wealth to a few lucky nations or class warriors. He rid the company of all its enemies, even friendly ones, built the enterprise to a state of perfection, establishing a global corporate empire that could have run forever in peace and harmony if it had been managed properly.

But that was the one thing he didn't do, the single aspect of management that very strong executives often find it impossible to accomplish was choose a fitting successor. Tiberius, Livia's grouchy, perverted, vicious offspring was next up, and the one after him was worse, and so forth, until we have to ask ourselves how this great corporate entity survived its own senior management for so long.

# 10

# The Spirit Fails

Well, that's about it. From here on in, we have about five hundred years any self-respecting operation would be proud of, but it was pretty much the same-old same-old: the occasional senior management team that wasn't rife with psychos and morons built on the achievements of the past and left us some very nice art and excellent arches in a lot of surprising places, although nothing comparing to the amazing collection of literary and architectural genius that marked Augustus's day. No matter how well they did, they were humming the tune laid down by the big boys in days gone by. And they acquired too much, exposed the company to too much risk, tried too hard.

The bad ones, and there were some cosmic jokes among them—quite a few, actually—used the empire as their personal toy, overextended it stupidly, raped and pillaged where they should have left well enough alone, buggered sheep and close relations, and generally screwed things up in such a way that,

eventually, Rome, Inc. could not be fixed as it was then consti-
tuted, and was forced to move its headquarters half a world away
and completely change its infrastructure from secular to religious.

Quite often, these interstitial Caesars were funny, or at least
what happened because of and to them reads like some kind of
gag whipped up by Poe, or Terry Southern.

The good, the bad, the many, many ugly ones, what are they
to teach us about management, leadership, the creation and
destruction of power, the strategic realities of corporate life?
That people as clinically depressed and sadistic as Tiberius make
very poor senior managers? That if you, like Nero, set fire to the
place you're supposed to be running, even for a very good personal reason, people may hold it against you?

Being CEO is rarely what it's cracked up to be, as individuals
as disparate as Dennis Kozlowski, Kenneth Lay, Lou Gerstner, Al
Dunlap, George Westinghouse, Jack Welch, Steve Case, Dick
Grasso, Michael Eisner, Jerry Levin, Bill Clinton, or Al Capone
and many others would be happy to tell you, those who are alive
or available for interviews. And after Augustus, well, it was defi-
nitely a high-risk post, with deplorable job security, and a very
Pyrrhic exit package.

Let's look at the record. Antony should be counted as one of
the guys who ran the show for a while, because he did just as
surely as Martha ran things from the joint while she was on her
little vacation. We know what happened to him. Tiberius was a
miserable bastard who liked to be served at his feasts by naked
teenagers who would disport for his pleasure. Not that there's
anything wrong with that. He did many other obnoxious things,

too, mostly due to his amazing ill temper that descended into madness when he was forced by Augustus and Livia to divorce the woman he loved, the mother of his children, and marry the whorish daughter and fellow victim of Caesar's notion of family values, the horrendous Julia. Tiberius hated Rome, hated humanity, hated his mother and his wife. The best that can be said about him is that he hated being Caesar as well. After a certain point he left corporate headquarters and never came back, preferring to hang out in Malibu. Who was going to stop him? He was Caesar!

Toward the end of his reign, he was joined by a young fella who knew how to show an old soldier some respect. After he came around, things perked up a bit, although the old guy started feeling rather poorly all of a sudden. After a while, he was dead.

That young man was Caligula—Gaius Julius Caesar Germanicus for short. He started out the pet of the army, which had loved his father, Germanicus, who I really should have told you more about, one of those terrifically popular officers, very successful in the field, who just die a little bit too young to earn anything but the cover of *People* and the love of those who read it. For a while, Caligula was bizarre and newsworthy, like Ted Turner in his prime. Then he went completely nuts, routinely had sex with his sisters, sodomized everything in sight, killed a fair number of people, but of course that was par for the course. He was just crazy, and when he started having his horse elected to public office and placing statues of himself in the holiest temples, he was murdered by officers of the Praetorian Guard, who presumably saw their duty as the protection of Rome, as opposed to its senior officer.

Claudius, who looked so cute in the PBS series, was murdered by his wife Agrippina so that her son Nero would succeed him. That's not nice. On the bright side, Claudius was responsible for the acquisition of Britain and the founding of Londinium, which later became London, but that's another story.

Then came Nero, fabulous Nero, sort of a combination Mick Jagger and Idi Amin Dada, another utter psychopath who was forced to commit suicide by the Roman Senate after a variety of entertaining depredations you can enjoy in the work of Suetonius. He murdered his mother. 'Nuff said?

Then we have Galba, who was assassinated after seven months on the job, like one of our recent popes, I hear. Be that as it may, Otto, who succeeded hapless Galba, did even worse. He committed suicide after ninety days as Caesar, or so the spin goes. One can speculate otherwise. Things must be really bad to kill yourself when you're Caesar. I'm thinking he was helped along in some way. Vitellius, the next lucky duck, was murdered too.

Vespasian, a very good operator and handsome fellow, runs the place well and is succeeded by Titus, another CEO of good repute, except, perhaps, to Jews, who remember the destruction and sack of Jerusalem, their capital, in 70 A.D., and the beginning of the diaspora that sent them to places as far-flung as Londinium, where they begin the practice of thinking Yiddish and dressing British, which later helps them in America.

After that, there followed some others who are about as interesting to me as, say, Jeff Immelt. They weren't murdered. They did okay. If you're addicted to more stories of triumphal acquisitions and new product integrations, there are about two tons of books at your local Barnes & Noble on the subject. Yes, there was a plethora of ongoing grandeur, no question about it, as I'm sure there will be at Microsoft after Chairman Geek is gone. But for students of management, it just isn't the same.

As the years went by, for every Trajan and Marcus Aurelius building and perfecting and doing all that terrific stuff (unless they were being terrific all over *you*) there were a bunch of nutty nonentities that should, by all rights, have laid the empire low almost immediately. Murderers. Drag queens. Pathetic, sniveling weasels. A reading of the last thirty Caesars or so generates a single pertinent question: *Who?*

True, the army, the Senate, and a host of other special-interest groups had diminished the importance of the CEO position in the global behemoth that was Rome, Inc. in the days before it spun out and died. But looking at the developing mess that was Roman leadership for half a millennium, the real issue we should probably wrestle with is not only what produced the fall of the corporation about five hundred years after Christ appeared in the land of the Jews, but also what in the world was keeping it together? Certainly not its senior management!

For anyone who works for a living today, the answer is simple, when you really think about it. There are quite a few components to the equation, but they all boil down to this:

It was good to be a Roman.

And to be a middle manager when the corporation was in full swing? It wasn't just good, it was the best job the world had to offer. Nobody who was gainfully employed and receiving benefits from the organization wanted it to go down. You were a player in the greatest city on the planet, working for the very best company, with the greatest expense account and access to technology the world had to offer. Everywhere around you were Jews, Greeks, Syrians, Spaniards, and Celts, even those hairy, violent Germans now and then, all with their noses to the grindstone in the everlasting pursuit of success. No employee of Time Warner on his way to the restaurant du jour ever felt half as good as the Roman vice president on his way to dine at the cool agora bistro of the moment, where he had a very good couch near the central pillar. No investment banker holding a breakfast meeting in the Sony private dining room high above Madison Avenue could be more pleased with himself than the commander of a Roman legion as he awoke on a Grecian isle that was now his personal province.

The world was a line extension of the family business. You could travel to just about anywhere, pursue your agendas, be they commercial, financial, or military, picking up friends and trading partners everywhere you went. That's why Rome was such a melting pot of all the cultures then extant—at least the ones that were at peace with the company. Money, goods, and ideas flowed into and through the corporate culture, enriching it, fortifying it, and, in the end, mixing it up so badly that a new unifying principle had to be implemented.

It was middle management that kept the corporation going. And if the senior officers of the company were running around naked in pursuit of goats, or disemboweling Christians for their amusement, or killing five innocent hippopotami with one blow of their mighty sword, who really cared? Let the big boys do what they liked! As long as the organization produced income, housing, career opportunities, and the best quality of life the world had ever seen? So what? Being one of the guys in charge of that particular show was the best possible alternative for a long, long time, even if there were the inherent dangers of fire, death by hacking and slashing (or being thrown from a cliff), or the virtual certainty of being yanked out of the metropolis every now and then for a trek to some godforsaken corner of the world where there was no decent coffee. The hell with the bosses. But the gods bless Rome!

Life was good, as good as it had ever been in any civilization, ever, even counting Greece, which was very glorious but not always so comfortable. Food was better here, too. It is possible to get kind of sick of lamb.

More to the point, starting in the final years of the Republic, there were suddenly quite a few people around you'd have to describe as rich—not just the chosen few who sucked around the aristocracy, but others, too. And with wealth came access to a very nice life, not as simple and austere as things were in the old days, and a lot more pretty, and fun, too.

A great number of people were still poor, of course. Shame about them. They lived in squalid tenements jammed into the seedy parts of town, where the plumbing wasn't quite up to snuff and the danger of fire was omnipresent. It was always possible that these poor would band together to make a very great nuisance of themselves, which was why, from the late Republic forward, the corporation found it advisable to provide the populace with free grain, which in turn made it necessary to acquire and hold far-flung entities—such as Egypt—which provided it, much as it might seem wise to certain strategic planners of our day to see that our empire has perpetual access to fossil fuels, even if it means going to war to accomplish those ends.

In addition to food stamps, the company also provided a host of ongoing conflicts to keep the potentially fractious young men busy, and a full schedule of entertainments and games to assure a general mood of revelry and continued amusement in the populace.

And if you had a little bit of money—well, there was nothing like Rome. There were new fabrics you could buy in the streets, and perfumes that drove your nose wild with sensuous delights, and jewels from the four corners of the empire, and foodstuffs from odd places, and writings you could read in Greek and even, increasingly, in Latin. What a town.

You needed money to live, of course. Real estate values, particularly on the slope of the Palatine Hill, went crazy and stayed there. Then as now, location was the key factor, followed by location and location. City villas, like the one purchased by Cicero from Crassus, went for nearly two hundred thousand sesterces! Can you believe it? Where was this world headed to? But those city mansions paled beside the suburban estates the big corporate players maintained out where the air was just a little bit sweeter, the schools were better, and you had some distance from your neighbors.

The commuting Roman would deal with his trip to work much as you or I might today if we lived in Pound Ridge or Glencoe.

The ride in would be accomplished either on horse or by chariot, depending on whether you wanted to get some reading done, I guess. The vehicle (or animal) would then be parked in places designated for that purpose. Really rich guys would then pick up a litter to carry them the rest of the way, much as executives I know will jump in a limo for a trip of three or four blocks, especially when it's hot and the car is cool. Others would walk. At the end of the day, you would pick up your transportation and head back home.

On the weekends, or whenever you wanted to get away from the stabbing, hacking, and daily poison of political life in the big city, there were pretty places along the Adriatic, on the Greek Islands or the Amalfi Coast, just like today, only without satellite entertainment. As a Roman, everywhere you went you were welcome. It was better than an American Express card. Nobody ever was declined, if they were wearing a toga.

It wasn't all plums and dancing around the maypole. Your average Rome, Inc. middle manager was a hardworking cog in the machine. He rose early, with the sun, and had a little breakfast—perhaps a hunk of bread dipped in wine or, for those who were not late-stage alcoholics, honey, with some cheese and fruit. His wife then stayed home to spin and deal with household issues, for the working world belonged to men, ostensibly. The truth is, so many of the robust, hairy fellows died in the prime of their lives—killed in a war, stabbed by bad guys in an alley, tossed off cliffs by a drunken mob, you name it—that many of the crucial duties of civilized life actually belonged to the women. But they never told the men anything like that, while they were presiding over everything in typically Italian fashion, so today we hear a lot about how the men ran everything. Which, for the most part, they certainly did, as long as they lived.

The industrious Roman citizen worked throughout the morning, and his duties, as ours, depended on his trade or his position within the infrastructure. There were paper-pushers who checked incoming goods at the port of Ostia while others heaved them from ship to shore and still others haggled about the margin between wholesale and retail. There were men in construction, naturally, since the city was always building itself up, repairing old structures, doing teardowns of useless ones, furbishing and refurbishing—stonemasons and designers and engineers and diggers and those who provided drink and meat for the laborers. The markets teemed with all kinds of goods and services, and the bars kept a lively trade going in whatever libation you might desire, mostly wine.

Wine was the drink of the people. Tiberius, in addition to his other great virtues, loved wine so much that the populace gave him a nickname. Instead of Tiberius Claudius Nero, they referred to him as Biberius Caldius Mero—he who drinks hot wine with no water added. Let me know when you stop laughing.

Then came lunch, called *prandium* (hence the notion of the postprandial nap). It was a rather light meal (Caesar salad?) that might include a few leftovers from yesterday's ridiculous, disgusting, gluttonous, hyperattenuated dinner.

Then it was back to work for a while.

If you were a member of the aristocracy, you were pretty much limited to one of three professions—the army, politics, and law.

This functioned to put a lot of talented people in those fields, with the least impressive probably opting for the latter, don't you think? There was excellent crossover between the military and politics, with a great career in the first virtually guaranteeing success in the other.

Those among the blue bloods with no taste for any labor at all could attach themselves to a functioning noble, who would then be their patron. Their "work" consisted of waiting in the morning for the day's handout of money or food, and then going to while away the rest of the daylight hours doing nothing, or taking a bath, which was a very big deal for these, the first slackers in recorded history, but certainly not the last.

As opposed to the classy class, the progeny of working people had the whole panoply of professions open to them—even politics, as we have seen from the careers of self-made men like Marius. Many went into their family's business, whatever it might be, or the army, which was also a meritocracy, but there were quite a few other professions, from medicine to architecture, chosen by normal people and even liberated slaves, who were called freedmen.

They worked. They partied, which consisted, a lot of the time, of public entertainments that are as impossible to understand today as the frenzy around a tie score in the World Cup would be to your average NBA fan. They prayed to their gods. They relied on their local Human Resources Department or, lacking that, the state, if the bottom fell out. Doesn't sound all that alien to us, does it?

After about 4 P.M. on the old sundial, the working Roman,

man and woman, went someplace to relax and kibitz about the
world situation, their crazy bosses, and the events of the day just
past. They had plenty of taverns and watering holes, many of
them filled with actual water, but for them the public baths were
their equivalent of a drink after work, although it is a rare corporate player indeed in this century who gets to enjoy his martini
stark naked with his jocular coworkers, thank God.

Dinner began as evening came in, and lasted, depending on
your wealth, until the moon was high in the sky and you simply
couldn't retch another bite.

They did not sit for this, the central social event of the day, but
reclined on pillows, picking this and that off the platters as they
were presented, since eating utensils as they now exist were
unthought of. There were usually three main courses, starting off
with a round of appetizers that would put your average corporate
cocktail hour to shame—eggs in a variety of forms, salads, veg-
etables with dip, some escargots, perhaps, or, if you were very
lucky indeed, the delectable favorite—roasted, stuffed dormice,
which for those of you unschooled in rodentia, are basically ham-
sters. Yum-yum, huh? No question.

The main course, of course, was meat. Meat was followed by
more meat, which was then chased by a selection of meat.
Sometimes there was fish, but that was only because fish was
considered a form of meat. They had veal, beef, wild boar, suck-
ling pig, venison, hare, wild goat, porpoise, mackerel, mullet, oys-
ters, chicken, duck, goose, partridge, thrush, dove, even, for
those truly seeking to impress, flamingo and ostrich. Ostriches
were readily available from the Colosseum, where it was consid-

ered great good fun to shoot off their tiny heads with special arrows.

For dessert, the sated crew would enjoy a nice piece of cake, or some pudding—or cherries and dates for those who were on a diet.

It's nice to think of these, our progenitors, enjoying themselves like a crowd of hungry salesmen at Peter Luger every night, particularly since they had no scotch, eschewed beer (so barbarian), and had to prepare these feasts without the benefit of sugar, potatoes, tomatoes, or coffee or tea. They didn't even have bread until the second century B.C.—before that they ate a form of mashed-up corn gruel. It just goes to show you that people can have a good time anywhere, as long as the company is good.

Around 100 A.D., during the time of Trajan or perhaps a little bit before, when things were going pretty good after years of insane Caesarean management, Pliny the Younger, a friend of Suetonius and very much a man of the world, had occasion to visit with an elderly Roman gentleman who had come to the time of life when one represents the very best a culture can produce. He came away moved and impressed.

I do not think I have ever spent a more delightful time than during my recent visit to Spurinna's house; indeed I enjoyed myself so much that if it is my fortune to grow old, there is no one whom I should prefer to take as my model in old age, as there is nothing more methodical than that time of life.

In the morning he keeps his couch; at the second hour he calls for his shoes and walks three miles, exercising mind as well as body. If he has friends with him, the time is passed in conversation on the noblest of themes . . . What glimpses of old times one gets! What noble deeds and noble men he tells you of! What lessons you drink in!

After riding seven miles he walks another mile, then resumes his seat, or betakes himself to his room and his pen; for he composes, both in Latin and Greek, the most scholarly lyrics. They have a wonderful grace, wonderful sweetness and wonderful humor, and the chastity of the writer enhances its charm. When he is told that the bathing hour has come— which is the ninth hour in winter and the eighth in summer— he takes a walk naked in the sun, if there is no wind. Then he plays at ball for a long spell, throwing himself heartily into the game, for it is by means of this kind of active exercise that he battles with old age.

After his bath he lies down and waits a little while before taking food, listening in the meantime to the reading of some light and pleasant book. All this time his friends are at perfect liberty to imitate his example or do anything else they prefer. Then dinner is served, the table being as bright as it is modest, and the silver plain and old-fashioned: he has also some Corinthian vases in use, for which he has a taste but not a mania.

The dinner is often relieved by actors of comedy, so that the pleasures of the table may have a seasoning of letters. Even in the summer the meal lasts well into the night, but no one finds it long, for it has kept up with such good humor and charm. The consequence is that, though he has passed his seventy-seventh year, his hearing and eyesight are as good as ever, his body is still active and alert, and the only symptom of his age is his wisdom. This is the sort of life that I have vowed and determined to forestall, and I shall enter upon it with zest, as soon as my age justifies me in beating a retreat.

This is what the hardworking, educated, decent Roman could aspire to. Is it any wonder they were willing to go to the ends of the known earth to protect its borders and bring all that goodness to others—even if they didn't want it?

The possibility of such exquisite self-perfection was very real to these citizens, not just to the rich, but also to quite a few working people, even those who had once been slaves. This made it easy for the majority of Romans to buy into the system, no matter how badly they were doing at the time, and to support, for the most part, the conservative actions of the most entitled classes.

There was also the great myth of the Corporation itself that unified nearly all people under its enormous theological, philosophical, and emotional umbrella. This was a unity that held for a long time, fraying at the edges and eventually unraveling altogether when the center began to lose its grip on the minds and hearts of a people grown increasingly diverse—geographically, racially, and linguistically.

For while the everyday life of the corporate enterprise was going along swimmingly, and the people had every reason to be content and excited about their place in the scheme of things, there was an emptiness creeping at their core, something sick in the Roman spirit. Into that void rushed a number of alternatives, and then one, which in the end supplanted everything.

The Roman faith was a simple one. Pagan, whatever that's supposed to mean. I know people who believe in Ouija boards and wood sprites and attend a Unitarian church. Others in our day attend gigantic worship/consumer complexes that combine huge church spaces with all the comforts and entertainments of your local mall. People believe a mix of all kinds of things, particularly now, it seems. It's tough to determine whether the original Roman religion was deficient or lunk-headed in any way. It brought them great good fortune for about twelve hundred years.

It was built on a belief that the gods—and there were many, with a wide variety of temperaments and capabilities—wanted what was best for Rome, and that a very special relationship existed between the state and the powers that ran the universe. Just as the Jews believed they were the chosen people, Rome believed that when thunder cracked across the sky, it was speaking to them.

The founders of the corporation, including Romulus, were supposed to have been descended from the gods themselves—in his case, Mars, the god of war. Others, like Julius and Augustus Caesar, started human and ended up as gods, which wasn't simply an honorific. People prayed to them. Their prayers were probably answered about as many times as are ours when we offer them to our unresponsive divinities today.

Every household had its presiding deities that conferred blessings on all under the roof, particularly the father of the establishment, who was, in his small way, considered the god of the household he had established. Ancestors were worshiped, as were other members of the dear departed. This led them to treat their old people very well. There were no nursing homes, because Dad lived in the back room upstairs and shuffled down in the evening for a glass of hot wine and a game of dice with the kids.

The gods communicated by a variety of silly means to these backward pagans—through the way the guts of animals aligned themselves in a fire, and how they burned; how birds circled and dove; how the rain came in, in mists or torrents, on the morning of a battle. Augustus, for his part, always liked a little drizzle before a day's fighting. He felt it was good luck. They believed in luck, and in fate.

There were certain things that were seen as expressions of what was good in the eyes of the gods, and what was good for Romans. Simplicity. Hard work. Respect for certain family values. The responsibility of men to take care of their families and the state. Simple food. Harsh punishment for enemies, boundless generosity toward friends. Humility before the eyes of the gods. All the people—except for certain celebrities—were expected to conform to these norms.

Apparently, as we have seen, it was also okay to kill people in pursuit of the needs of the state, in pursuit of any sort of acquisition or corporate restructuring, your enemies, the friends of your enemies, the enemies of your friends, pets, wild beasts from Africa, and, if you were a senior officer of the company, just about anybody who got on your nerves. As brutal and violent as this world is today, this is one area where Rome wrote the book. It's a little more difficult to kill people today, although Viktor Yushchenko, the president of Ukraine, has the bad skin to demonstrate that there are still people around who believe that it's advisable to do so when you're in a hotly contested election.

This confluence of superstitions and beliefs was celebrated and practiced in hundreds of temples large and small throughout the corporate empire. This system aligned the fate of Rome with the spiritual life of its citizens. There were certainties. They made men comfortable in the horrendous acts they had to perform every day in the name of the enterprise. They made women rest somewhat easier when their children went off to battle, because it was for the city and, by extension, its gods. The concept of the corporation was intertwined with its employees' view of how the universe was constructed. What was good for Rome was good for everyone in the world who mattered, and good with the forces that ran the spirit world as well.

Then Rome, Inc. grew, grew to include millions of people who didn't share the way of life of those who ran the operation, including a fair number of recent acquisitions whose employees were hostile to it. Then, after a while, those who ran the business from the very top seemed to forget the simple, direct, underlying spirit that brought the company together, the big circle in the dirt that Romulus, the original creative genius behind the myths that made these people One, carved into the dirt, the circle that created the mystical division between Us and Them. They got corrupt. They fell out of touch with the gods, and with the people. The gods might be cruel and tough at times, but they couldn't possibly approve of this string of ridiculous pederasts who ate until they fainted, and killed their own mothers and stepchildren.

And what of all these other, powerful faiths that were sweeping through the Mediterranean from the east? What were our bourgeois, corporate soldiers, and matrons to think of those? Some of them were wild! Crazy Jews! And these Christians!

Just as the soul of the people began to waver, as the idea of Rome and the machinery of the universe fell out of sync, a host of the already acquired subsidiaries in the north began a protracted effort at a reverse takeover. Some who had previously been content to leave the company alone began to look at corporate headquarters with a gleam in their eye—because their business was acquisition, too.

Germans perched in the north. Those obstreperous Parthians continued to press in from the east, along with other hostile armies swooping in across the steppes from Mongolia. Each would have to be conquered, thrust away from the center, in spite of their incredible vitality and determination. Thousands, perhaps hundreds of thousands, would have to die. And for what? For Rome? But what if Rome no longer had a deal with the gods? What if, in fact, these other gods were better?

The locus for the greatest sense of spiritual malaise, quite naturally, was the Roman army, probably because intelligent people who are called upon to slash and hack others to death frequently need an extremely potent and reliable ethical and religious underpinning to do so. After a while, the military, unwilling to trust in the demented perverts back at home, began to take responsibility for naming, supporting, and then, if necessary, killing the chief executive, which proved as unreliable a method of executive recruitment—and decruitment—as any.

It is instructive to see who the army felt comfortable with, and the kind of individual who emerged to fill the considerable leadership gap that was developing in the executive suite of the corporation. A lot of these chief executives, when they flipped out, revealed the intense desire to fill the spiritual gap widening in the Roman psyche—by transforming themselves into gods on earth.

In 180 A.D., for example, Commodus, the son of the excellent emperor Marcus Aurelius, swept into Rome on the back of the army after the death of his father, probably of plague, but back then who knows. He was nineteen, and had held the ceremonial title of Caesar since he was five, which might not have been too salutary for his mental health. Kids are grandiose enough without having that kind of high-octane fuel screwing up their sense of proportion.

He started well, making peace with the northern tribes and doling out perks to the multitudes. Before long, however, he started dressing like the god Hercules, which may have been hard to triangulate, because really, who knows how Hercules dressed?

Anyhow, things went pretty much immediately from bad to worse. The new emperor's notion of godly dress devolved into wearing lion skins and carrying a club. This was bad enough. In the fall of 192, he officially declared that he was, in fact, Hercules himself.

While the Roman aristocracy was generally somewhat dismayed, the people were willing to give their new god a fair shake, if he could prove himself. Like us, they were always willing to be entertained by their famous nutcases. So Commodus set out on a strategy to prove his Herculean nature by appearing in the

Colosseum and battling everything from dwarfs to hippopotami in most heroic fashion.

How low had this show fallen?

This crazy megalomaniac, perhaps working on the advice of highly paid consultants, would actually enter the arena and battle the most skilled of gladiators, who "lost" to him and were then spared. He also killed innumerable animals, since, you know, he was Hercules. Toward the end of his run, he declared his to be the "Golden Age," lest there be any doubt. Which, of course, there was. He also named the months after all the various positions he had attained during his reign. For some reason, those names didn't stick.

And now we get into the region occupied at this time in world history only by the maniac hair-transplant candidate, Korea's Kim Jong Il, who has dubbed everything from the nation's largest amphitheater to its major highways to its smallest urinal for himself. Commodus proceeded to crown the legions who fought for Rome "Commodianae," and the fleet of warships that clogged its harbors as the "Alexandria Commodiana Togata," and the Senate was graced with the new name of "Commodian Fortunate Senate," and his palace and the Roman people were all given the name "Commodianus." The day he announced these impressive name changes was forever to be called the "Dies Commodianus." As a crowning touch, after a fire hit a portion of the city, he took the opportunity to reestablish the place under the catchy new name—that's right—"Colonia Commodiana."

Fortunately, before things got completely out of hand, a gladiator and wrestler (who must have been very good-looking, since his name was Narcissus) strangled the Caesar in his sleep. Rome became Rome again.

This didn't solve many problems, though. Things hit bottom less than three months later, when the Praetorian Guard—the Secret Service of the executive suite, established by Augustus to protect the CEO against all threats—assassinated the emperor Pertinax, who is memorable solely for that fact.

That wasn't so bad. They'd done that before in the name of Rome. But this was different, and far more seedy. At a loss for a successor, convinced (rightly) that it was they, not the chief executive, who actually ran the place, the Praetorians actually auctioned off the job of Caesar to the highest bidder, a forgettable, affluent senatorial doofus by the name of Didius Julianus, who got his just reward sixty-six days later, when he too was assassinated.

At this point I'm thinking it was better to be in middle rather than senior management at that stage of corporate development. Immediately thereafter, the Senate disbanded the Guard, which lowered the paranoia level at headquarters quite a bit, but didn't do much about the quality of the leaders being selected by the true powers in the empire—military, political, mercantile, whatever was floating the collective boat at any given moment.

Heliogabalus, for instance, appeared a few years later in 218, hoisted to the top slot by the military, which liked him until they got to know him. When he became CEO, he was just a teenager. He entered the city in full regalia, dressed as the Syrian sun god. Ruled by his mommy, he did pretty well for about five minutes. Then his cross-dressing and mad crushes on unsuspecting gladiators ran him afoul of the people, the army, which was too butch to really enjoy reporting to a preening transvestite, and any politician who was even vaguely awake. Folks really were grossed out when he forced a vestal virgin to marry him. The defilement of the sainted virgin was bad enough, but this was compounded by the fact that, prior to desecrating this holy, unsullied maiden, the young man had shown limited interest in any woman at all. After a short time, he was killed too, hunted down and beheaded by soldiers who found him hiding, with his mother, in a latrine. So much for that god.

There was a huge hole in the heart of Rome. As this kind of nonsense was going on, increasing numbers of people were turning east, thinking about the words of a carpenter who had died on the cross some two hundred years before, and converting to Christianity, embracing a faith that taught its adherents to turn the other cheek at the exact moment when the Vandals, Visigoths, and Huns were heading into town with their own plateful of agendas.

# 11

# The Decline and Fall of the Roman Empire (Abridged)

The early Christians were an unpopular lot. They were cheery when you tortured them, and refused to curse you when they died. They sometimes sang when they were being transported to their deaths, and worst of all, they were talking about this Jesus all the time. Sophisticated Romans certainly paid due respect to the gods, but they didn't get all misty-eyed and go on and on about them. They had too much business to do.

The worst thing about these pesky fanatics was that they refused to do two things that lay at the heart of the well-being of the corporation—they refused to add all the good old regular gods—Jove, Venus, Mars—to their own new one, as civilized peoples did under the Pax Romana, and they refused to pledge allegiance to the emperor. This would be like failing to sing "The Star-Spangled Banner" at a Yankees game, only much, much worse.

Theophilus of Antioch, later named a saint just as the great

Caesars once were, said it humbly, but pretty firmly. "I shall pay homage to the emperor," he said . . .

> . . . but will not adore him; I shall instead pray for him. I adore the true and only God, by whom I know the sovereign was made. Well now, you might ask me: "Why don't you adore the emperor?" The emperor, given authority by God, must be honoured with a proper respect, but he must not be adored. You see, he is not God; he is only a man whom God has placed in that office not to be adored, but in order that he exercise justice on earth. In a way this authority was entrusted to him by God. As the emperor may not tolerate that his title be taken over by those subject to him, so no one may be adored, save God.

Not only was this kind of thing highly offensive to any good Roman, it was treason. To place anything above the state and its divine leadership? People were thrown off a cliff for a lot less. Any citizen in my corporation who starts taking God over the chairman isn't long for my world, either.

So decent Romans understood why it was important to persecute the Christians now and then, as a state policy. And they did—crucifying them, boiling them, killing them in their halftime shows. From our vantage point in history, we take a dim view of this aspect of the corporate personality, as well we should. We would never torture dangerous members of a fanatical religion that is anathema to our way of life. Certainly not throw them to lions.

There were many other excellent reasons for deploring the nasty Christians, if their anti-Roman attitudes weren't enough for you. They were faithless heathens, you know, and very lazy, too. Also, they ate their babies, and sometimes each other, in stew, usually. It was part of their religion. Not only that. You know the flood last year that just about spoiled all the crops? Christians did that. Also, they somehow put a whammy on the entire port of Ostia last winter, when so many people's tongues turned black and they died.

In the year 35, the Senate decreed the new religion to be "strange and unlawful." That's quick. Christ died in the year 30, didn't he? That's really speedy for an institutional reaction. Both Tacitus and Suetonius, two very intelligent men with a snarky eye for hypocrisy and cant, were engaged to slag the Christians, the former finding the religion "deadly" and "hateful," and the latter somewhat more moderately agreeing that it was "harmful."

Serious annoyance of Christians followed, but not constantly. It was an on-again, off-again thing, sort of like how the Cossacks dealt with the Jewish shtetls in nineteenth-century Christian Russia. And throughout the enormous corporate empire, word began to spread that the old gods were dead, and the new way of looking at things provided a nice alternative to the constant grinding of private and public enterprise, and the continual hacking and slashing of people who were your brothers under the eyes of heaven.

That drill went on for a while, with CEOs of the west-coast operation getting smaller and stupider all the time. Sometimes the emperors were just kids, sons of somebody with some marquee value, thrust into the corner office by one special-interest group or another. These had to be "helped" by powerful second and third bananas, as is often the case with any weak chief executive. This decayed culture fosters henchmen and elevates toadies and other forms of reptilian life to very senior roles indeed. I've been there, and I can tell you that it's worse than working for a straightforward despot any day.

Henchmen have no soul . . . so we're back to that spiritual rot again. Here are all these soulful Christians running around saying basically what everybody knows—that the fish stinks from the head and that only a fool would worship a fish head.

Enter the single most important executive in the new millennium (or the old one, I guess, from our vantage point). Constantine transformed the corporation entirely, made the powerful new faith the state religion, moved the corporate center out of harm's way, and basically shut down operations in the west, leaving it to its fate as a variety of extremely un-Christian hordes horded down on it. He was so important that the next seven CEOs after him called themselves Constantine. That's powerful branding.

Constantine's dad was a Roman executive of the old stripe, who had worked under Diocletian and then taken over in the title of Augustus, which was a good one, but not the tippity-top. The young Constantine was a good commander, and won the respect of the army in the east and also against some truly ugly foes, the crazy Picts, who at that time were led by some brave heart even more unpleasant than Mel Gibson.

Upon the death of his dad, Constantine was instantly hailed by the army as the new CEO, came back from Britain, and set-

tled in Trier, which was not Rome, which itself is pretty interesting. It's clear at this stage of history, the year 306, you didn't need
to be at corporate headquarters to run things. That tells you
something about the fungibility of the corporate center, not just
emotionally, but operationally as well.

In 312, Constantine fought off a rival Caesar at a battle just
as crucial as that which had taken place at Pharsalus nearly four
hundred years before. You don't need to know where it was or
what the other guy's name was, any more than you need to know
who ran against FDR in 1936. This contest left Constantine the
clear number one in the west-coast operation. Perhaps more
important, the night before the battle, the young king had a
dream in which he was commanded to emblazon the shields of
his men with the sign of the cross. When he won, as you can
imagine, his feelings about Christianity had enjoyed a significant
alteration. In 313, he and the top east-coast guy, Licinius, issued
what has become known as the Edict of Milan, which made it as
good to be a Christian as to be an old-school pagan, and supposedly ended all persecutions. They continued for some time anyway, but only for entertainment purposes. The steam had gone
out of that game.

Afterward, Constantine began to use the religion as a shield
behind which he stood in many political conflicts, and even
though he didn't get baptized until late in life, he was now with
the faithful. It was good he had this spiritual fortress, especially
when he killed Licinius, who was now his brother-in-law, and
Licinius's son, who was his nephew, too. Later on, he ordered the
execution of his own son, Crispus, and the mother of three of his

children, Fausta. It's good to have God on your side when you're doing that kind of thing.

From 324 on, Constantine was sole ruler of the whole business on both coasts, which was a very big change for the company at that time, which had labored under an east coast/west coast split even worse than that suffered by Disney in the 1990s.

As soon as he controlled the whole operation, he modestly declared that the ancient Greek city of Byzantium would be renamed Constantinople and become the new corporate center. By 330, major improvements in the physical infrastructure had been accomplished, and Rome was now demoted to the status Albany now enjoys as the capital of New York State.

Constantine was in many ways a terrific chief executive, interested in both the spiritual and political improvement of his subjects, and very worthwhile for continued and more detailed study, which I encourage you to do elsewhere.

We're going to move back to Rome, or what was left of it, where Christians were turning the other cheek all over the place, local leadership had been thoroughly relegated to the backwater, and a sustained attack on the former corporate center was under way that can only be compared to the threat posed by the Carthaginians long, long ago. Except back in the Punic Wars, as Hannibal crossed the Alps and wave after wave of enemies smote at the heart of Rome, Inc., there was leadership that was at one with the gods. No matter how many times you put the old Rome, Inc. down, back they came, until you were just too exhausted to fight anymore. You didn't mess with the corporation back then.

Now there were bozos who provided very little direction, no vision, and were powerless to retain management control over the many far-flung acquisitions and operations with which previous generations of grandiose executives had burdened the corporation. And the army was as rife with peaceable converts as anywhere else.

And look at these adversaries. "Bar bar bar," is what their language sounded like. So that's what they got called.

There were Germans. Even back when they were wearing animal skins, they had a great work ethic and, according to Tacitus, a strong moral fiber in comparison to the divorce-happy, adulterous Romans. They started moving in around the time Commodus was slaughtering innocent mammals in the ring. There were the Goths, which included Ostrogoths from the east and Visigoths from the west, who did really, really well, and succeeded, behind their great leader Alaric, in being the first to sack Rome since the Celts did it in 400 B.C. For three days, they did their sack dance. Then they left and went back north, where they encountered the Franks, and then there were the Vandals, who also got as far as Rome and had a party there, then receded to their kingdom by the Rhone.

All these bad barbarians were driven forward and down to make their way throughout the western empire by the same inexorable force—the charming, alarming Huns, under a senior officer whose public relations effort matched the efficacy of his day-to-day operations, Attila, or, as he liked to be known, Attila the Hun, to differentiate him from all the other Attilas. Friends called him the Scourge of God, but they were probably just sucking up. To this day, with plenty of competition, he's still the world's most recognized barbarian.

Contemporary observers describe this prepossessing fellow as a pleasant-looking individual—graced by an enormous head, a complexion tanned by the sun, tiny beady eyes, a big flat nose, and a few scraggly hairs where a lush, sensuous beard might have been on an Italian countenance. He also apparently liked to roll his eyes in his head with great ferociousness, to enhance the whole terror thing he was going for on the available audience.

Like the Mongols, the Huns were a smelly bunch, possibly due to their diet of raw meat and their hairy clothes, which reeked of the fat that kept them conveniently water-repellent. Cast your mind back to the days when the cultivated Etruscans had to deal with the crazy Romans swooping down, reeking of wine, blood, sweat, and lust. Now the sandal was on the other foot, and all these raggedy-ass competitors, formerly content to writhe under the Roman yoke, were all over the map, taking away the corporation's market share from Britain to North Africa. And these Huns? They were the worst yet. Other barbarians called them barbarians.

The Big Hun himself was born in 406. The quality of leadership that distinguished him from other vicious bastards during his days in the fifth century was that he was the most brutal, terrifying warrior in the known world—a post once held by whatever Roman was in the neighborhood. No more.

When he was very young, just an adolescent, he was traded as a hostage to Rome during some peace negotiations. He stayed there for two years. You have to think he got a taste for city life.

How do you keep them down on the steppes after they've seen the Forum?

In his twenties, he went at the Visigoths, who were no cream puffs, and laid waste to everything in his path. Laying waste, in fact, was his corporate mission, and nobody was better at it. He got over on the Ostrogoths, too. No Goth went unturned. Later on—shades of Romulus!—he killed his brother to take sole control of the Hun throne, which was a movable object, obviously.

You can feel how ineffective the Roman military was against this inexorable threat. In the east, Theodosius paid tribute to the Huns so they would stay away and focus on the west, which turned out to be a pretty smart strategy.

Attila kept at lesser barbarians, and always maintained focus on his ultimate objective—Rome. Each season, he swept into one juicy region or another, acquired booty and territory for his relatively small pop-and-pop operation. To be fair, this was no different than the first three to four hundred years of Roman history, was it? Back then, it was our guys wearing the heavy leather. Now the truncheon had passed to a new generation of beast.

Like the Carthaginians before him, Attila just kept at it, winning a few, losing sometimes, always advancing toward his objective. In 451, about half a million men thundered down through France and headed directly for the poor, corrupted heart of the aged organization, sacking and dancing over some of the great cities of Europe. When he needed to, Attila could lay siege to a town, which was unusual for a barbarian horde, most of whom were generally content to swarm and that was pretty much it. Everywhere they went, they triumphed and showed the Roman world who was boss.

With the help of the Visigoths, which shows you how truly horrendous things had gotten, the western empire was able to keep the Huns at bay, at least that year. This alliance is doubly interesting when you look at the chronicles of that day and realize just how many barbarians were now in positions of influence and power in the bosom of Rome, Inc. It must have been like working for Time Warner after the AOL merger.

Things worked out about the same for Rome as they did for Dick Parsons and crew, although it was touch and go for a while. The next year of 452, Attila and his tallow-greased lunkheads were back again for another merry season of pillage. It almost got them all the way there. Then tragedy struck—in 453, while planning what would be his final and triumphal campaign on Rome, the great Hun died at the age of forty-seven. It was the night of the feast celebrating his marriage to a beautiful and much younger woman—his seventh wife, by the way—and after a night of drunken Hun sex, he keeled over and died of a massive hemorrhage in his nose. He could have been a music industry executive, but with inferior health coverage.

In retrospect, as he fades somewhat disgustingly from view, we must admit that the Hun himself was not in any way a gorilla, in spite of his rolling eyes and delicate temper. And he was not devoid of wisdom. Here are a few of the things he was purported to have said before that last, fatal nosebleed:

- Great leaders never take themselves too seriously.
- In a political war, watch your back.
- Only make enemies on purpose.
- Perception is reality to a Hun.
- Those who appear to be busy are not always working (the secret of highway construction crews to this day).
- You are not remembered by what you did in the past, but by what people think you did.
- Every Hun is responsible for shaping his life circumstances and experiences into success—no other Hun, and certainly no Roman, can do for a Hun what he neglects to do for himself.
- Some Huns have solutions for which there are no problems (I know at least six guys who have made this their job description).
- Suffer long for mediocre but loyal Huns. Suffer not for competent but disloyal Huns.

None of these are particularly brilliant. But all are more sagacious than we might expect from a yak-breathing warlord.

If this philosopher and mass murderer had not been so heartlessly taken from us at that time, Rome, Inc. might have fallen to the Huns and we could move along right now to our stirring conclusion. But once again proving that corporate leadership does matter, the sons of Attila turned out to be about as effective as the sons of Henry Ford, and the Hun threat dissipated. Their descendants are now forced to live in Hungary, which seems punishment enough.

The west-coast office was a pathetic stump of its former greatness. The corporate center, such as it was, had moved to the

pleasant little town of Ravenna, and it was all over but the shout-
ing, and of course a little more killing and fighting. The western
empire was dead, but it kept on twitching, and for Rome, Inc.,
even at the end of days, that spasm of the phantom limb perforce
involved a battle over control of the executive suite, even if nothing at all worthwhile was going on there.

The last CEO, Romulus Augustulus, or "little Augustus," was
crowned in 475 at the age of ten. He was a puppet of his father,
Orestes, who was really running what was left of the operation as
the military commander in Italy, until he was killed by Odovacer,
a barbarian mid-level executive who had some bone to pick with
him.

Romulus was allowed to live, possibly because he hadn't even
begun to shave yet and presented no threat to anybody. He and
a big retinue of hangers-on and senior management without portfolio were exiled to Lucullanum, the retirement villa occupied by
that old dyspeptic, Tiberius Caesar. That castle had certainly
seen better days, with prepubescent lovelies of all races and
sexes frolicking between the legs of all those depraved old
geezers! Now look how the mighty corporation had fallen.
Barbarians were kings. Romans were Christians. The action was
in Byzantium. It was all over.

In 476, little Augustulus abdicated. All that was left of the
great Rome, Inc. in the west was a small stand that sold Italian
ices on the steps of the Pantheon. It is still there.

# Afterword

# What Have We Learned?

In 1096, the united army of the Roman Catholic Church, a force that transcended nationality, or rather asserted religion as a common nationality, descended on the Middle East for a variety of trumped-up reasons. I'm sure they seemed good at the time, as the rationale for all wars shines with the luster of righteousness until that glow is rubbed off by the perspective of time and emotional distance.

We're not here to debate the Crusades, however, as tempting as it might be to do so as our global empire now faces off with another medieval force convinced of its own righteousness. What is important here, in our examination of what became of the first great multinational corporation that was Rome, is that some six hundred years after the fall of its original, brilliant incarnation, it had reformulated its mission, recast its organizational structure, redeployed its capital and other resources, and was doing fine.

The Roman Empire did not fall. It simply did what all corporate entities do if they wish to survive over centuries and millennia—it reinvented itself and emerged as a highly organized, spiritually unified, highly politicized, and enormously wealthy new global entity, one that continues to thrive to this very day. It's called the Roman Catholic Church.

This great corporate reorganization came flying out of the box as early as the fourth century, when Constantine made Jesus the new Jove and moved the center of the company from the west to the east coast. In those early days, the Church, which had suddenly become the corporate culture any smart person got their arms around, simply took on the organization and leadership characteristics of the empire it ostensibly served. When that controlling secular entity was gone after the abdication of little tiny Augustulus, the Church was left standing. From that time forth, the new sacerdotal corporation just maintained its own flow under the structure that had served the empire, which could no longer subsist simply on structure alone. They gave the boss a new title and got down to business; business of a different kind, true, but in many ways similar. The warriors, sales weasels, architects, mendicants, assassins, party animals, merchants, and politicians who swept around the world, acquiring new territory and producing wealth, did so under a variety of flags. But all that activity was united, as it had been for more than a thousand years, by the spirit and genius of Rome.

There are many empires that came after, but the children of Romulus and big Augustus are still spread across the world, from the tip of South America, across the ancient cities of Europe, into Asia and back to these great United States. Rome continues to rule vast chunks of our landscape, its line-officer priests reporting to middle managers of increasing size who in turn must account to senior and executive vice presidents of cardinal size who themselves fear that phone call from the top dog, who may be Polish or German or Nigerian at any particular moment, but who will perpetually reside, with his court, in the heart of the city that was built by an earlier, and admittedly less celibate, Caesar.

The question for us, a civilization facing challenges not unlike those that faced our progenitors in the dangerous days of, say, Marcus Aurelius, is this: How did this ancient culture—without cell phones, BlackBerrys, or corporate jets to obviate the vicissitudes of travel—manage to survive for so long and, in the end, transform itself into another iteration that was almost equally successful?

The answers may be helpful to us, both as corporate citizens and as citizens of this increasingly perilous planet. Some of the strategies and solutions suggested by our Roman ancestors are not always pleasant, but—as Attila himself was known to have said—let's resist the urge to kill the Hun who bears the message, no matter how unwelcome it might be.

First, Rome lived because it was blessed with a series of highly effective, creative, vicious executives. Never in the history of humankind, before or since, was there a group of senior executives and middle management that, over an extended period of time, combined simultaneously a massively powerful creative drive with the willingness to kill people by whatever means were available. Today, most of the great senior managers I know have a potent admixture of those two seemingly contradictory forces. If you possess only one, however, you may do well for a while, but your reign will not be sustainable.

If you have to choose between the two, keep this consideration foremost in your strategic mind: corporations willing to kill
people do better than those which are not. Executives with the
same capability are more successful than those without it; the
most scary, mean mothers do best, then and now. If innocent
people run in terror when they hear your name, you're probably
on the right track. That said, history shows that it pays to be reasonable. It's generally bad practice, for example, to kill your
friends and family, or screw them either literally or figuratively.

At the same time, it is obviously unwise to allow your enemies
to live. Brutus spared Marc Antony after the death of Caesar
because he didn't want to do the "wrong thing" in pursuit of the
higher ideal he was demonstrating as he stuck the shiv in his
longtime friend and mentor. Soon after that, Antony came back
and crushed him. More new executive teams than you can count
have been derailed by the former power crew coming back to bite
them. A good proscription is the best beginning for a strong leadership cadre, and subsequent quiet executions to maintain order
among the guys whose salaries are in the annual report isn't a bad
idea, either. That's often fun as well.

With all obnoxious people sent to early retirement, the corporation may then move forth under the banner of a good chief
executive. But that presence alone is not enough. When things
were working well, all classes within the Roman corporation
were balanced, with each having its own muscle and will to use
it. Pampered patricians, sweaty plebes, hardworking bourgeoisie,
a burly haute executive branch—all worked together to put forth
a common agenda, at least as far as the rest of the world was con-

cerned. While Rome might always be fighting among itself, the Family always showed a united front to subsidiaries and potential acquisitions.

What we have seen is that greatness in middle management and a happy, productive employee base is only to be found in an organization that is graced with a strong center and some level of common respect among all parties for the big guy in the corner office. Sadly, he (or occasionally she in the case of a Cleopatra, Martha, or Carlie) is not as easy to find as one might think, and in a diseased culture is nowhere to be seen.

On the bright side, the leader does not need to be an Augustus, or even a Caesar, to earn a gold plaque at day's end. They do, however, have to be about something other than executive privilege—making money, eating too much, getting laid, screwing the shareholder, having million-dollar parties featuring statues that pee real vodka, or soaking the organization for your $12,000 shower curtain or greens fees. The chief executive must, like Romulus or Caesar or Augustus or Constantine, have a vision of what the organization is all about, and move without hesitation or guilt to make that vision a reality. It helps when that concept of the corporation is not repulsive to the moral and ethical sensibilities of the people who work for and serve the corporation, or those who might be acquired by it.

Speaking of moral and ethical sensibilities—our investigations reveal that many people appear to have them. This includes even powerless employees who are supposed to do what management tells them and shut up about it. You can't get rid of those scruples, either, no matter how hard you try. So if you're an organization that seeks to endure beyond the life of the latest despot, that means providing some kind of spiritual underpinning that folks large and small can feel good about. This ethos must be able to release the workforce from any prior moral constraints they may have felt against killing, looting, salting fields, laying waste, falsifying earnings, cutting the benefits of long-term employees, or plucking out the occasional eyeball.

And while a powerful executive may confer much spiritual absolution in this regard, only when the prevailing God or gods are with the program, rendering what we do inherently right and proper in the eyes of the forces that run the spirit world, will the organization have the full and cheerful participation of all its citizens.

This unity between the corporation and the universally accepted notion of what is Good is essential going forward. If you don't have it, all kinds of reprehensible behavior previously approved by your culture becomes suspect. Without it, you can't be mean to animals, slaves, strangers, the disabled, and people who don't share your religion, for instance, without feeling very uncomfortable about the whole situation every time you go out to dinner and a show. After a while, all that screaming and dying gets on your nerves. You might even feel that the gods will be angry with you for some of the things you do both at home and on the road. It's only a short step from that to running away in battle.

With good leadership, a happy middle-management cadre, and employees who think the gods are smiling, though, the corporation might go on forever were it not for one inevitable liability that will, someday, almost certainly lay it low: the specter of continual growth. Today, Wall Street presses all organizations to grow or lose their buy status. Yet growth comes with a terrible price. Good acquisitions—ones you can manage for growth and wealth—are the lifeblood of any enterprise. Bad acquisitions, contrariwise, are the parasites that suck off the lifeblood of a working enterprise. It was the reach of Rome, far exceeding its grasp, that in the end taxed even its awesome capability to keep things calm and productive under the tent.

You have to move forward and grow, because it gives a large number of indolent people who would otherwise get restive something to do—lawyers, investment bankers, murderers, turn-around artists, ditchdiggers, caterers, foot soldiers, senior officers with an unsatisfying portfolio in existing operations. But too much of this particular sweetmeat is bad for the digestion. You can only gluttonize on so much. Then it starts coming back up.

Diffuse, overextended, the central idea of the corporation watered down by myriad influences and a cacophony of beliefs and voices, the company flails. The problems you used to solve now overwhelm you and all the Huns who used to perch at your gate in frustration march down Main Street in their tutus and weird hats. They don't knock when they come for you and your silverware.

Worse yet, perpetual growth and acquisition can only be purchased by continual war. This is a Pyrrhic price. At some point, the company must reach a point of stasis, even if the Street penalizes you for insufficient rapacity. There is a time for conflict, certainly, and you never want your guys to get soft or insufficiently hungry. But a couple hundred years of peace never hurt anybody, either. It's even good for business, boosting genuine internal revenue growth and new product development, opening reliable shipping routes and lines of communications and making people happy in pursuit of the good life.

Finally, the core of longevity for any great enterprise is clear. From the earliest Roman enclave of mud huts on the banks of a little backwater called the Tiber to the announcement that Apple is moving to an architecture based on the Intel chip, the key to eternal youth is the ability to transform.

Rome started as a family business, run by a guy willing to murder his brother and steal his neighbors' women. At its height, with all pistons firing and the machine humming at full speed, the Roman Empire engineered a peace that brought the whole world—except, perhaps, for those nasty, stubborn Parthians!—together under a single grand idea that, at the time, was better for most people than any other. It was a beautiful place, too, the Roman world, with fragrant gardens, gorgeous buildings, and a middle class whose lifestyle was not all that different from ours. When that concept of the corporation grew old, unworkable, and too dangerous to have fun in, it mutated one last time into the enormous financial and religious edifice that today shepherds 1.1 billion souls and runs more spaghetti dinners worldwide than any other.

I work for a very large corporation that is the descendant of one that made nuclear power plants that itself grew out of a manufacturing company that made transformers and what it fondly referred to as large rotating objects. Today, we make content. Our company has offices on every continent. Our revenue is growing nicely, and our margins are good. We suffer, of course, under the shadow of many challenges, including the disruption that the global situation could impose on our business, the movement of market forces we can't really control, and the demand from Wall Street for continual expansion and growth, no matter what idiotic form that expansion may take or the cost it may impose on the structure and integrity of our organization. Some of our leaders are terrific. Others should be in Phoenix.

The best I can tell you is that it's still fun to be in middle management. My friends in other corporations feel the same way, pretty much. The names on our buildings are different, but we all know that we work for Rome, and the way the empire goes, so go we. We get nervous about the state of the big show now and then. But we don't really sweat it too much. What's the alternative?

It's still the best game in the world.